2. Count Pali Pálffy

6. Dr Arpad Plesch

5. Mr Deering Davis

Horses & Husbands

HORSES AND HUSBANDS

The Memoirs of Etti Plesch

Edited by Hugo Vickers

THE DOVECOTE PRESS

First published in 2007 by The Dovecote Press Ltd
Stanbridge, Wimborne Minster, Dorset BH21 4JD

ISBN 978-1-904-34954-9
© Hugo Vickers 2007

Designed by The Dovecote Press
Printed and bound by Biddles Ltd, King's Lynn, Norfolk

All papers used by The Dovecote Press are natural, recyclable products
made from wood grown in sustainable, well-managed forests

A CIP catalogue record for this book is available
from the British Library

1 3 5 7 9 8 6 4 2

Contents

Introduction

BY HUGO VICKERS

LONDON society is not easily taken by surprise, but in the early 1950s the arrival of Dr and Mrs Arpad Plesch on the London scene was a moment to be reckoned with. Coming from the heart of post-war Europe, with its economic crises and the lingering aftermath of wartime, the sudden appearance of the Plesches did not pass un-noticed. They established themselves in a series of suites at Claridge's and remained there for the duration of the season. Outside the hotel, which was not unused to large cars, there stood each day a dark green Rolls Royce, with magnificent lantern headlamps.

Soon afterwards Arpad and Etti Plesch gave a magnificent party to launch *her* daughter and *his* step-grand-daughter (and step-daughter) into London society. There was a ball for seven hundred and a seated dinner for fifty-six, to whom caviar was served as the first course.

In 1961 Etti Plesch pulled off an enviable coup in winning the Derby. And she did it again in 1980, thus becoming the only woman in the two hundred year history of that great race to win the Derby twice. The Plesches will long be remembered as unusual figures in the racing world. Today the scene is different. It was remarkable that these victories could be won by relative newcomers and won with such panache and style. Etti's daughter, Bunny Esterházy, duly married into a well-known aristocratic family of Scotland with the Queen and Princess Margaret as guests at the wedding.

There were many stories about the Plesches, and questions

7

asked about who they were and where they came from, most particularly relating to the wartime activities of Arpad Plesch. As Etti Plesch herself often said: 'The English are very suspicious of money, especially if they don't know where it comes from.' In this long-awaited book of memoirs, she answers some of these questions.

Until her death in the spring of 2003 Etti lived in Monte Carlo, retained a flat in Paris, and travelled to London, New York, Baden Baden and to other fashionable places such as Jamaica according to the season of the year. To meet her in the last years of her life involved a delicious lunch at Claridge's or the Connaught. She enjoyed a healthy appetite and this was matched by the many hoops through which she put the waiters during the lunch – frequently a litany of complaints when the service or cuisine failed to live up to her exacting standards.

Etti was a fund of up to date stories about the glamorous figures of many lands and her memory stretched back into the early years of the 20th century. She relayed these stories in tones that were a wonderful mixture of the alert, stern, friendly and then rather Germanic.

For many years Etti's friends urged her to write her memoirs. At last, in the 1990s, she did so. There were some amusing adventures along the way to publication. In 1998 Eleanor Lambert, the doyenne of publicists in America (who lived to be 100), forged an introduction between Etti and a distinguished editress. I accompanied Etti to her office, many storeys up a New York skyscraper, with panoramic views over Manhattan. As we sat down, Etti's mink coat settled into the chair beside her and curled up spontaneously, making itself comfortable like a dog in its favourite chair. It was a few moments before it was still.

At such a meeting, it is always a help to find a shared interest. The editress had lately become keen on horses.

'How many horses do you have?' asked Etti.

'Well, just the one.'

'Where do you keep him?'

'Well, he's in a field next to my house in Connecticut.'

'I see.'

There was a silence.

'How many horses do you have, Mrs Plesch?'

'I never had very many – eighty or a hundred, I suppose. Now I have maybe six or eight.'

'And they are in Monte Carlo?'

'No, of course not! They are everywhere – at Chantilly, in Ireland. You must come and see them. It would interest you.'

'Unfortunately I can't come to Europe. I have a little dog.'

'But you must book him a seat. Bring him with you on the Concorde!'

Somehow the two ladies were not talking the same language, and though it was disappointing that no publishing deal was forthcoming, there was an element of relief at the avoidance of future differences of approach and interpretation.

Etti's is an unusual story. She came from an almost medieval style childhood in Austria, surviving six marriages and becoming a major figure in the equestrian world. She writes with disarming verve and courage, and relates, amongst others, the story of how she lost two of her husbands to the same *femme fatale*.

In her early life she loved a young man whom she was not allowed to marry. Here, I feel, lies the key to her later life. Thwarted in this, she embarked on numerous adventures, bringing to each a certain resolve, but moving on – without looking back – when circumstances dictated. Finally, in her marriage to Arpad Plesch, she was able to turn the experiences of her past into the way of life for which her ancestry had prepared her.

Etti died aged 89 on 29 April 2003. By that time most of her memoirs had been completed, certainly enough to publish. As editor, I have added a few notes here and there to help the reader, and added occasional biographical details for some of the key figures in the story, since Etti did not concern herself greatly with matters that had but tenuous connection to herself.

I have tried to keep my interruptions to the minimum. Where they do appear, they are rather like the recitative in an opera – moving the story along, and filling in the background. Yet I have not hesitated to add to the story where I feel there is more that can be said. There are two particular instances that immediately spring to mind – Louise de Vilmorin and Dr Arpad Plesch. Only after Etti's death did I manage to penetrate the Bibliotheque Jacques Doucet to read the letters between Tommy Esterházy and Louise, while a kind friend in America unearthed some fascinating F.B.I. files on Dr Plesch. I have also added biographical entries for each husband so far as that is possible, to make it easier to follow Etti's marital progress.

I concede that had Etti published these memoirs in her lifetime she might have chosen to edit out some of this material, but I am equally sure that these discoveries will add immeasurably to the story, and give the readers a fuller picture than might otherwise have been possible.

I am grateful to Etti's daughter, Countess Bunny Esterházy, for her interest in the progress of this book and for lending photographs from her mother's collection. Also to the Hon Mrs Simon Howard, who before her marriage, worked closely with Etti for some weeks and also undertook independent research; to George Sayn for his original introduction to Etti and his encouragement throughout the project; and to the enthusiasm for it of Prince Rupert Loewenstein, and the late Baron Alexis de Redé, both of whom keenly urged publication. Dame Frances Campbell-Preston kindly recalled her own experiences with the Plesch family as a patient of his brother, John (Janos), and remembered them as far back as the 1930s. Alexander George, a great-nephew of Arpad Plesch, contacted me after Etti's death, and was again encouraging. I am grateful to him and to his mother, Susan George, for their help in matters relating to the

Plesch family. Diana McClellan kindly tackled the F.B.I. and launched Freedom of Information Act requests to unearth the files on Arpad Plesch, adding considerably to our knowledge of him.

I would also like to thank Richard Jay Hutto, author of *Crowning Glory – American Wives of Princes and Dukes,* for his help in identifying several elusive fugures, the American Philosophical Society in Philadelphia for help with the Ulam family, the Chicago Historical Society for an attempt to track down the death of Deering Davis, Nikki Manwaring for pinning down the death of Michael Ulam in Monte Carlo, Etti's former chauffeur, Franco Bruzzese, for taking me to visit the Arpad Plesch mausoleum in the cemetery at Monte Carlo, Michael J. Arlen for information on his aunt, Daria Mercati, and Viscount Norwich for permission to quote from his parents' letters to Louise de Vilmorin.

Etti's book is enjoyably devoid of sentimentality or political correctness. She lived into an alien age, where the standards of her day had been allowed to lapse. Hers is not an English story but a cosmopolitan one. It is, I believe, a unique one.

HUGO VICKERS
July 2007

Prologue

RECENTLY I was in London, lunching at the Connaught. The man at the next table was eating caviar. I have to tell you. I did not envy him. His caviar was *black*. This seemed to me typical of life today, in which so few high standards are maintained. There is no good caviar today. The best caviar I ever ate was at the wedding of Karim (the Aga Khan). It was grey – with just a hint of pink.

Everywhere, life is unpleasant. Paris is crowded and noisy, London is dirty. Monte Carlo is over-run with tourists. The Prince* has done a wonderful job for Monaco. He will hand it over greatly enriched, but for me living there, every expedition is a kind of nightmare. When I walk out of my building, I am right in front of the great Casino. These days there are just tourists, badly dressed, slouching about. It is all so unlike the days of my youth when everything was invested with an aura of glamour and excitement. Here, on the same terrace, the men would gather daily in the season for the pigeon shooting. Dressed in their Edwardian suits and hats, invariably sporting magnificent moustaches, they stood with their backs to the Casino and fired at the pigeons.

What is the matter with chefs today? They do not know how to prepare food and the waiters do not know how to serve it. I don't know where to go. Sometimes I think I will go to America and find a home in Palm Beach. There the service is good. There is always a man who comes to fix the swimming pool and it is

---

* Prince Rainier of Monaco (1923-2005)

possible to get things done.

Travelling becomes increasingly fraught with hazards. I can't take the train through the Channel Tunnel as there are no porters. Recently my friend, Alexis de Redé, was on the train, and, believe me, he does not travel light. When he arrived in Paris there was no one to take his suitcases. So Alexis told them that he would not get off the train until a porter came. They told him there were no porters, and so he just sat there. Eventually they had to find him a porter.

In my long life I seem to have lived several very different lives. I have known great hardship and unhappiness, but, despite all this, I remain an optimist. I know that in life you have to keep going. It is the only way.

I am glad to have the chance to write my memoirs. This book has had many adventures along the way. Apparently mine is an unfashionable story, because it does not fall into the mould of stories of great suffering. But I feel it is of interest and young people might like to know something of a world that is past. Few now remember the days of the horse-drawn carriage. Few have travelled as widely as I have, or made their homes in so many different lands.

ONE

The Derby

HORSES have always been the passion of my life. I had dreamt horses ever since I was a child. The long hours that I had spent at my grandmother's Slovakian castle, Napajedla, had given me more than a good grounding. My grandfather, Aristides Baltazzi, won the 1876 Derby with *Kisbér*, which he partly owned with his brother, Alexander. The race was watched by Queen Victoria and competition from the English horses was very strong. *Kisbér* won by five lengths, ridden by Charlie Maidment, and the two brothers earned about £100,000.

I had always longed to have my own stable and stud and to race and breed my own horses. Somehow other matters got in the way. It was not until I had married my sixth husband, Arpad Plesch, that my dreams became reality.

We were keen to live an interesting life together and Lord Willoughby de Broke suggested we buy a racehorse. I needed little encouragement. Arpad knew nothing about horses, but he always said I could x-ray a horse with my eyes. So we decided to buy a mare and try our luck.

Arpad was very intelligent. Whatever he turned his mind to was a success and now he turned his mind to the business of breeding. He created something called the Parabolic Index. In earlier days, the *Sporting Life* used to publish the measurements of those horses entered for the Derby. Arpad worked out a system by which you divided the horse's height by its girth and then divided that figure by the result of the hip to hock measurement. This reached a figure and the lower that figure was, the better chance you had of finding a good horse.

I remember that at my daughter Bunny's* wedding he explained this system to the Queen. I remember also how annoyed the owners of the yearlings at the yearlings' sales were when Arpad's man came forward with his tape measure to assess the horse. They did not know what he was doing, and they did not like it.

In 1954 we bought several yearlings at the Newmarket sales. Among them was *Stephanotis*, who won six races, including the Cambridgeshire Handicap.

In 1955 we lunched with Madame Couturié at the Haras du Mesnil in Normandy. She had an Italian chestnut mare in her paddock, called *Dinarella*. Her owner seemed to have lost interest in her and had not paid his bills. I liked her so we bought her on the spot for just under £3,000, a reasonable price. Shortly afterwards we were lunching with Aileen Plunkett at Luttrellstown, her romantic Gothic castle in Dublin, and met a friend of hers called Captain Tim Rodgers. He remembered that the Dollanstown Stud was for sale.

We went to look at the stud and fell in love with it at once. We knew we had to have it. But the then owner had promised it to Godfrey Davis, of the car hire company. Aileen said: 'If you really want it so badly, you must go outside and sit in our wishing chair and wish like mad.' So we sat in the chair. We were able to buy it. *Dinarella*, who had been living at Middleton Park Stud, now had a home of her own.

We had a good stud farm, and in Bob Griffin a good vet. He had been the manager at Dollanstown since 1941. When we bought Dollanstown, it consisted of 400 acres. Next to it we bought an extra 100 acres so as to keep some paddocks ungrazed. This helped to ensure that parasites, which are such a danger to a horse, died out of the ground.

Arpad chose Harry Wragg as trainer. He had been a successful

---

* Etti's daughter, Countess Marianne (Bunny) Esterházy, married Hon Dominic Elliot, younger son of 5th Earl of Minto, in May 1962. They had two sons, and were divorced in 1970.

jockey for 27 years, and was so good at timing his challenge that on the Turf they nicknamed him 'The Head Waiter'. People have now forgotten that in London the cockneys used his name 'Harry Wragg' to rhyme with a 'fag' when they wanted a cigarette. He went on to be a great trainer, and when the old Aga Khan, for whom he had trained some winners, heard the choice, he was impressed and told Arpad: 'It was the best decision of your life.'

To begin with, in 1956, we had all this land and just two mares! The other was *Lady Sylvia*. And then there was *Dinarella*. We had great luck with this mare. She was crossed twice, first producing *Thymus*, who won the Poule d'Essai des Poulains (the French 2,000 Guineas) and then went to stud in South Africa. Then she was crossed with *Pardal* and produced *Psidium*.

Gradually we built up the stud so that by 1963 we had thirty-nine mares, some rather expensive, others remarkably cheap. We had shares in seventeen stallions. Each alternate year we raced in either his name or mine, using the same colours – light blue, with scarlet spots and cap – the original Baltazzi colours from the century before.

Derby winners don't come by chance. Arpad calculated that to win a race of 2,600 yards by just ten yards is superiority of a mere quarter of one per cent. Thus no mistakes must occur. In 1961 the horses were racing in my name. Arpad gave *Psidium* to me to race in my colours, as he felt I created the right atmosphere for him. We liked his mother *Dinarella* as she came from the great winning family of *Pretty Polly*. There was good Italian blood and good conformation. *Psidium's* father was *Pardal*, the French sire.

A Derby horse needs a top-rate jockey. We were thrilled to have the Frenchman, Roger Poincelet, riding for us. A jockey must accept riding instructions from the trainer, and he must bring back accurate reports afterwards. Poincelet was a cold, imperturbable character, who did not lose his head.

A lot of this is common sense, but one missing element can lose the day.

THE EPSOM DERBY

There are many great races in the annual calendar, but somehow, even today, none of them have quite the impact of the Epsom Derby. It is the gem of all the classic races, and the race is run on the most testing course in the world.

The Derby was first run on 4 May 1780 when it was worth £1,125. The race came about as a result of a roistering party at the home of the 12th Earl of Derby, during which Sir Charles Bunbury dreamt up the two races – The Derby and the Oaks, the second race being named after Lord Derby's Epsom home. The Derby was for three-year-old colts and fillies and the Oaks for three-year-old fillies. So important did the race become that in the nineteenth century Parliament was suspended on the day of the race, and during the Crimean War the results were recorded in 'general orders'. It is said that Bismarck once told Prime Minister Disraeli: 'You will never have a revolution in England so long as you keep up your racing.'

There have been some famous occasions in the race's great history. The Prince Regent won it in 1788, King Edward VII won it three times, twice as Prince of Wales with *Persimmon* and *Diamond Jubilee*, and then as King with *Minoru* in 1909. And the Aga Khan won it four times, or five if you include his half-share in 1948. The Earl of Rosebery was the first Prime Minister to win it in 1894 with his horse, *Ladas*, thereby fulfilling his schoolboy triple ambition of marrying a Rothschild, becoming Prime Minister and winning the Blue Riband of the Turf.

In 1913 the race was disrupted in the most shocking way when the suffragette, Emily Davidson, threw herself in front of King George V's horse, *Anmer*, an accident which brought the horse down, injured the jockey, and killed Miss Davidson – stupid woman. And so dangerous for the horses.

Each year King George V followed his father's tradition by giving a Derby dinner for members of the Jockey Club at Buckingham Palace. This altered the history of Britain, when, on the night of the 1920 dinner, Queen Mary took her sons over to a ball given by Lord Farquhar at his house in Grosvenor Square and there the Duke of York met Lady Elizabeth Bowes-Lyon.

The nearest that the present Queen came to a Derby victory was in Coronation Year (1953) when *Aureole* came second, ridden by Harry Carr. The winner was Sir Victor Sassoon's *Pinza*, with Sir Gordon Richards in the saddle.

I shall never forget 31 May 1961 – Derby Day. I woke early and was very excited. I ordered a light breakfast and took a couple of tranquillisers to calm my nerves. Later Arpad said it was a good thing I did not have to undergo a dope test! For the occasion I wore a green Balenciaga suit and my lucky amethyst brooch, which only comes out on very special occasions.

By ten o'clock I was ready to depart for Epsom, but Arpad appeared to be in no hurry, so I informed him that I was leaving now and would send the chauffeur back for him. It was just as well I got there early since my jockey, Roger Poincelet, spoke no English and my trainer, Harry Wragg, spoke no French. I was the interpreter as we made our plans for the day. Poincelet had never ridden in the Derby until then, though he had won the Oaks the year before. That morning, I walked the course with him and told him he must stay back in the early part of the race, because *Psidium* didn't like being close to other horses. He must drop right out and not move until the horses were in the straight. That is how Harry Wragg had won the 1928 Derby on *Felstead*.

Harry Wragg was quite encouraging when I went to see *Psidium*. He told me he had been working well and might well finish in the first five or six. At least he was more encouraging than Lester Piggott, who declined to ride him after his last race in France. Lester had come in fourth when *Moutiers* won the Prix Daru at Longchamps and said that *Psidium* was not a 'stayer'. Ten days later, sweating badly, he had run a bad race for Willie Smith in the Guineas, and Willie Smith said the same.

These negative reports prompted Harry Wragg to suggest we

dropped him from the Derby, but we were adamant that he should run. In the back of our minds was *Psidium's* performance in the 2,000 Guineas Trial in March that year, when he had stormed through from behind to come in third. Arpad told Harry Wragg: 'Pay no attention to the jockeys. Train him for the Derby.'

Arpad had still not joined me, so I lunched without him. I was worried that he must be stuck in traffic, but, resourceful as ever, he had instructed his chauffeur to tag in behind the royal party. Thus he whisked through the racing traffic. As ever, it was a wonderful sight to see the royal procession coming up the course. The Queen was there, with the Queen Mother, the Duke and Duchess of Gloucester and the Princess Royal.

In due course we made our way down to the saddling enclosure to inspect the twenty-eight runners in the field. I turned to Bunny and said: 'Oh I wish I would win the Derby one day!'

Bunny said: 'Well you certainly won't win it today, Mummy. Look at him. He's covered in sweat.' Some horses get very nervous before a race and *Psidium* was certainly sweating badly.

Meanwhile one man went round to a bookmaker and said 'I want to put £1,000 on *Psidium*,' and the bookmaker said 'I wouldn't do that. He hasn't got a chance,' and the man said 'Well just do it anyway.' The bet was made.

We went up to the owners' first floor balcony to watch the race. *Psidium* started right at the back of the field, way behind the solid mass of horses racing together. And there he stayed for the first eight furlongs of the race. He was still there as the horses came round Tattenham Corner. No one took any notice of him, but we could see that he was still right at the back.

Then suddenly, 150 yards from the winning post, he began his sprint and he was a marvellous sprinter, with so much energy, a lot of speed, tremendous speed. He ran so fast. I was so excited that I was shouting and screaming and Arpad, who had not spotted him, kept telling me to keep quiet. *Psidium* came round the other horses on the outside, right past the lot of them and he won. He had two lengths to spare. 66-1 he was. A complete outsider!

Hardly was he past the post than I rushed down the steep iron stairs to be with him. Arpad was left behind, and as I ran, I found myself weighed down by my heavy binoculars. 'Here, take these for me, please,' I yelled to a passing stranger, who was so surprised that he took them, and kindly returned them to me later. Then the Queen spotted me in the winner's enclosure. The crowds were calling out: 'Etti! Etti!' Then I was summoned to the Royal Box and the Queen asked many questions about *Psidium* and my grandfather's stables.

Meanwhile, there was one very unhappy bookmaker. The punter with the £1,000 bet returned to collect his winnings. The bookmaker asked him why he had backed that particular horse. 'Well I once knew a man who sailed on a boat called *Psidium* and I liked the name,' he replied. The bookie said: 'My God I wish you'd been in the *Titanic*!'

Lord Rosebery, who had been racing all his life and had seen seventy Derbys run, said he had never before seen such a race in his life, but even so he was a bit disdainful about a foreign winner. Then some people could not resist muttering unkindly: 'I wonder how many more pornographic books Dr Plesch will buy with the Derby winnings.'

On a happier note, there was an old lady of seventy-nine, who placed a bet of three shillings through the *Daily Sketch* newspaper, which bought tickets on twenty-seven of the horses. She won £5,507-10s on him, all for a bet of three shillings. There was great excitement in her village that night.

Our chauffeur also had some considerable calculating to do. Most of our staff had enjoyed a small flutter, and he was the man who had placed the bets and collected the winnings.

I didn't put a penny on him. I never bet on any horses. We had 130 at the time. Imagine if I bet on all of them! Both my trainer and myself didn't think he had a chance of winning. But I took home £34,548 prize money and the Gold Cup trophy.

Psidium was pronounced without the "P", so the commentators and cartoonists had fun. 'Pcheers', was the caption of Nicolas Bentley, while Peter O'Sullevan, commenting on my remarks about how beastly the press had been about my horse hitherto, wrote: 'Consider me in psackcloth!'

We had a party at the Savoy the same night. How do they do it in England? They had the whole room decorated with balloons in our racing colours, blue with red spots, by that evening. I was photographed being kissed by Suzy Volterra, who owned *Dicta Drake*, the runner-up.

It is fair that the owner should enjoy all these triumphs. So the horse runs a little faster than the others on the day, and the jockey is on special form that day, but it is the owner who oversees all the preliminary work and studies, and who bears the financial burden. We had aquired *Psidium's* mother when she was still carrying him. I had liked the look of the mother and Arpad studied her pedigree. We were both satisfied and the result was *Psidium* – our wonder horse.

Psidium also won the Grand Prix at Longchamp in 1961. Later he was at stud at Newmarket, and later still he was syndicated. He produced some stallions, a few of whom were winners, but none of them as good as him. Eventually he went out to Argentina. He was a disappointment as a stallion and therefore he is not remembered as one of the great Derby winners, but he won it.

Yet *Psidium's* triumph was memorable. The first three horses were all owned by women. His starting price of 66-1 was the longest for a winner of the Derby since *Craganour* was sensationally disqualified in favour of *Arboyeur* in 1913, running at 100 to 1.

What with winning the Derby and meeting the Queen, it was the most marvellous day of my life.

THE 1980 DERBY

I became quite well known in racing circles and sometimes at Longchamp, near the cheaper stands by the finish, I heard people crying out: 'Etti va gagner!' just as they often shouted: 'Rothschild va gagner!' It made me very proud. Our racing life kept us in England for long periods. I would have liked to have a house there, but we could not live in England for tax reasons. We stayed at Claridge's.

I had the great good fortune to win the Derby a second time, on 4 June 1980, with my colt, *Henbit*. I am therefore the only woman to have won that great race twice in its long history.

I bought *Henbit* for as little as $24,000 at the Fasig-Tipton Sale in Lexington, Kentucky, in 1978. He was bred by Johnny Jones, sired by *Hawaii*, who was owned by Charles Engelhard, the American businessman, who kept him in South Africa. *Henbit* was trained by Major Dick Hern, known in West Ilsey as 'The Major', a fine trainer. And on that day he was ridden by Willie Carson. *Henbit* was second favourite in the 1980 Derby and he was never further than seventh from the front.

Halfway down the hill to Tattenham Corner, Willie Carson looked as though he was in some trouble, but *Henbit* held sway and won at 7-1. But the victory was bittersweet, since poor *Henbit* limped into the winners' enclosure with a cannon bone broken in his off-fore leg. He broke it about a furlong and a half from the winning post, and it proved what a brave horse he was to carry on regardless. Dick Hern told the press that *Henbit* would not race again that season, and added: 'This injury to *Henbit* takes all the gilt off the gingerbread.'

The winnings that year were a mere £169,000, incredible when you think it was the richest race in the world.

It was funny to think that on the first occasion that I won the Derby, we had with us Henrietta Tiarks, now Lady Tavistock, attending her first Derby. In 1980 we had with us her son, Lord Howland, at his first Derby. Maybe there are some more members of the Russell family who have not yet been to Epsom!*

That Derby Day was memorable for another reason too. The weather was variable and looked as though it would be exceptionally cold. So I put on a thick woollen suit. Then, of course, the sun came out with a vengeance. I sweltered happily in full vision of the crowd.

As usual after the Derby, the winner is invited into the Royal Box to meet the Queen. I remember being greeted enthusiastically by Princess Michael of Kent, lately married into the family, who cried out: 'My cousin's won the Derby!' She claims to be related to me through her Windisch-Graetz relations.

At different times Arpad and I had horses in training with Sir Gordon Richards and Harry Wragg and also with various trainers in Ireland, France, Italy and America.

In 1962 Arpad decided to move most of his racing interests to France. He sent fourteen yearlings to François Mathet, who had recently ended his racing partnership with Suzy Volterra. And a few horses stayed with Harry Wragg at Newmarket.

It was Mathet who advised Arpad to buy two particular yearlings from the stable of an Argentinian owner, Monsieur Atucca, who had died. His advice was excellent since the two horses he picked from the large selection were both important winners. One was *Battittu* and the other was *Tapalqué*, who won me the Prix du Jockey Club in 1968.

THE VICTORY OVER *Nijinsky*

Sassafras was my best horse. He won both the Prix du Jockey Club in 1970 and the Prix de l'Arc de Triomphe the same year. This second race was memorable because everyone expected

---

* Henrietta Tavistock became Duchess of Bedford in October 2002, and her son Lord Howland became 15th Duke of Bedford a few months later in June 2003.

Nijinsky to win.

The 1970 Arc was run at Longchamp on Sunday 2 October. It was a fantastic day for me. François Mathet, my trainer, had advised me not to enter *Sassafras* in the St Leger, which was run about three weeks before the Arc. He said it would tire the horse and prove one race too many for him. So we did not race him then. But at Longchamp, he was in fine form, ready to run in the Arc.

It was funny that none of the racing press took the slightest notice of *Sassafras* in the saddling enclosure. They were all surrounding Charles Engelhard's Irish trained colt, *Nijinsky*, who had already earned his well-justified reputation as the greatest race horse ever.

I must say something about the opposition. Charles Engelhard was an American industrialist, the son of a self-made German immigrant, and Chairman of the Engelhard Minerals and Chemicals Corporation, whose three divisions refined and fabricated precious metals, dealt on metal exchanges and provided material for scientific and industrial purposes. He acquired control of various important users of industrial diamond abrasives. He was an imposing figure, as well known on the international social scene as in the world of finance. He made his mark in racing circles, having at the high point, some 250 racehorses in his name. Some of his great fortune came from ingeniously getting round South African restrictions on the export of gold ingots. He set up a local jewellery business called the Precious Metals Development Company, which ostensibly manufactured expensive jewels for export to Hong Kong. When they arrived there, they were melted down for their inherent gold value. Such was Engelhard's reputation that he was said to be the inspiration for Ian Fleming's celebrated James Bond villain, Goldfinger.

Nijinsky had earned his reputation by winning the Triple Crown in England, that is to say the Derby, the 2,000 Guineas and the St Leger, trained by Vincent O'Brien and ridden each time by Lester Piggott. *Nijinsky* was the first horse to achieve such a victory for thirty-five years. He also won the Irish Derby, a fourth classic. In fact, out of his eleven races, he had, so far, won all eleven of them. Lester Piggott's reputation as a leading jockey needs no repetition here, though personally I always thought that our jockey, Yves Saint-Martin, was a better rider.

The story of the victory of *Sassafras* over *Nijinksy* is invariably told as that of *Nijinsky's* defeat, endless questions asked as to why he failed to win yet again, rather than why *Sassafras* won. I see it the other way round.

It did not help *Nijinksy* to be surrounded by pressmen with flashing cameras before the race, as if he were a film star. Later, Lester Piggott complained that he had been badly placed in the draw – on the outside – but that is no excuse for losing. It seems that he failed to start his late run – his challenge – soon enough. And there is Piggott's own explanation – that he had a chance to go over to the rails at one point in the straight, but feared he might be disqualified by the French stewards.

We had a wonderful jockey in Yves Saint-Martin. Without him we would not have had our victory that day. The opening odds on *Sassafras* were 16 to 1, but he held his own and beat *Nijinsky* by a head. I still remember the great moment when Saint-Martin's arms were outstretched to the air in victory, a fantastic triumph, even if it disappointed the many supporters of *Nijinsky* who had flown in from every corner of the world. After the race, of course, we had all the press buzzing around *Sassafras*, while poor *Nijinsky* was alone and neglected.

It is sad that those who have written about the 1970 Arc take such a negative line. Claude Duval, the racing correspondent of *The Sun*, wrote mournfully: 'The Arc . . . probably saddened more people than any race in the history of the Turf.'

There is a curious postscript to all this. Charles Engelhard was mortified in defeat. I can never understand why grown men, successful in business and worldly-wise, get so upset and over-excited over a four-legged animal running in a race. Arpad had explained to me the tiny percentage by which any horse is likely to win, less than a quarter of one per cent!

Charles Engelhard stayed at the Ritz and he had a passion for Coca-Cola. Every night he ordered twelve bottles to be sent up to his room before he retired to bed. After his defeat in the Arc, he locked himself in his room at the hotel in floods of tears and he was not seen for three days. All he had with him to console himself were his bottles of Coca-Cola.

Nijinsky then failed to win the England Championship Stakes thirteen days later. After his second defeat, Piggott was heard to say: 'He is still the best horse I have ever ridden.' *Nijinsky* was put out to stud. Engelhard, who had bought him for £35,000, took nearly £265,000 in prize money, and then syndicated him as a stallion for £2,250,000 – a world record. But soon afterwards, the following March, Charles Engelhard died in Boca Grande, Florida, at the young age of 54.

It is funny to think that all my husbands survived the experience of being married to me and most of them remained friends. I didn't kill any of them, as *femmes fatales* are supposed to do – at least in novels! But I worry about Mr Engelhard sometimes. I know he was very stout and not healthy, but I do so hope I did not kill him. I am certain he died of a broken heart.

TWO

Background and Ancestry

I WAS BORN in Vienna on 3 February 1914. My name was Countess Maria Wurmbrand-Stuppach but I have always been known as Etti.

I am related to most of the royal houses of Europe, which I find intriguing, especially as I have trained myself to study bloodlines in my role as a breeder of racehorses. Family trees are complicated to explain, and best seen as a chart, but I can unravel some of the mysteries of my family.

The Wurmbrands were a noble Austrian family of ancient origin, one of the families 'mediatised' in 1806. Originally from Styria, a duchy in Southern Austria, they came to Ottomar, near Wurmbrand, and became seigneurs of Wurmbrand and Stuppach in 1130. The castle of Wurmbrand was built in 1200 and the title of Baron given in 1518. The family acquired the seigneury (barony) of Reitenau in 1580, quartering with their own the arms of the Barons of Zebingen through the marriage of Mathias I with Sybille de Zebingen. The Austrian branch of the family became Barons of Saint-Empire in Prague in 1607, Counts of the Austrian States in 1682 and Counts of the Holy Roman Empire in 1701. They were received into the Franconian College of the Counts of Souabia in 1726 and were hereditary members of the House of Lords of Austria.

My father was Count Ferdinand Wurmbrand-Stuppach. He married my mother, May Baltazzi, under rather strange circumstances. The wedding was due to take place in a church in Vienna, but two days before, the police got news that a bomb was hidden there, not to blow up my family, but to kill some members of the Imperial Family who were intending to be present. The wedding was postponed for a few days while a thorough search was conducted, and finally took place with an army cordon surrounding it. My mother, a notably brave woman all her life, was not in the least scared by this.

My mother was of Greek origin, the daughter of Aristides Baltazzi, who came to Austria as a young student and married a Countess Stockhau in 1884. It is through the Stockhaus that I acquired 'my royal past'.

My grandmother, Mitzi Stockhau was the great granddaughter of Princess Therese of Mecklenburg-Strelitz. She was the less virtuous sister of Queen Louise of Prussia, who made such a great stand in the Napoleonic wars, and Queen Frederika of Hanover. She was a descendant of Ludwig VIII of Hesse-Darmstadt. Other notable descendants of Ludwig VIII include Prince Rainier of Monaco and therefore his daughter, Caroline, and also her new husband, Prince Ernst of Hanover.

If you consider the father of Therese, Grand Duke Karl of Mecklenburg-Strelitz, then his sister was Queen Charlotte, who married King George III of Great Britain. This makes me a distant cousin of Queen Elizabeth II and indeed of most of the Kings and Queens of Europe, the majority of whom are descendants of Queen Victoria. Many other such connections can of course be made, but these blood-lines are enough to make the point.

Therese herself is the interesting one. My descent from her is through her extraordinary liaison with Count Lerchenfeld and not through her marriage to Karl Alexander, 5th Prince of Thurn und Taxis.

Therese was born in Hanover in 1773 and married Karl Alexander in 1789. She had one son and two daughters by him. But then Therese gave birth to at least one child by her eighteen-year-old lover, Count Lerchenfeld, and from this line descended my maternal ancestors, the Stockhaus. Apparently Therese had twelve children, some of whom were by Lerchenfeld, but she always managed to keep her husband happy and remain with him. There was a rumour that my maternal ancestor was in fact sired by Therese's brother, the Grand Duke of Mecklenburg, and apparently there exist some letters about this. At any rate the Emperor of Austria gave the child the title of Count Stockhau von der Muehl. The 'von der Muehl' part was chosen from the place where the Princess had her rendezvous and the child was born in a mill near her castle. Quite an amusing idea! At the end of her life Therese went back to live at Regensburg, in Bavaria, south east Germany.

The life of Therese is testament to the fact that I come from a powerful female dynasty. Therese not only had all these illegitimate children, but she succeeded in getting them ennobled. It was not as if she was a reigning monarch like Charles II of Great Britain or a ruling prince of Württemberg who could ennoble those of his descendants who married morganatically into Dukes of Urach or Princes of Teck, like Queen Mary's father. Therese managed to get her descendants by Lerchenfeld created Counts Stockhau, thus making them into a family in their own right with their own coat of arms – not totally unique but very rare in those days. The Stockhaus then went on to marry well and I descend twice over from them.

Therese also used her brains and extensive family connections to convert the lesser family of Thurn und Taxis from being very rich to gigantically rich. For some generations the Thurn und Taxis had been making their fortunes by modernizing the European postal services. Therese operated the levers of power as much as she could within her own world of Regensburg to gradually acquire control of the postal system in Europe. She was able to negotiate with the newcomers in politics, Napoleon in France and the Bernadottes in Sweden, as well as with old guard families such as the Metternichs. It is hard to know what we inherit in our genes or what we absorb by example, but much of the way that my family thought and operated could be traced back by an ingenious historian to the life of Therese of Mecklenburg. She had an instinct for knowing how to deal with the old establishment as well as powerful newcomers, who held power for a while.

My grandmother's alliance with the Baltazzi family was interesting in that the Baltazzis were a family looking for alliances. They moved in what would now be called the fast lane. They were dashing, good looking and had considerable panache. Coming from Greece, they were outsiders in Austria and their link with Austria was through an elder sister who married a new Austrian Baron called Vetsera, a name that will be forever associated with the Imperial family of Austria through the Mayerling tragedy.

The Baltazzis themselves had an interesting ancestry, very different from that of my Austrian forebears. Through their maternal families, they had an exotic international lineage in that they were half English. The Baltazzis were originally Venetian subjects who moved to Crete and settled in Chios. In the seventeenth century they settled in Constantinople or Stamboul as it was named under the Turks. They had a palace in the Phanar, the old Greek quarter, and another in Therapia, on the shores of the Bosphoros. (These two palaces were destroyed in the anti-Greek riots in the First World War. I saw the ruins when I visited Turkey in the last war – the coat of arms of the Baltazzis was still above the empty door frame – an arm with its fist holding a hatchet – a Balta). In the last century they also built a comfortable house in Pera, which is still there.

By the first half of the eighteenth century the Baltazzis were traders and bankers in Smyrna and this remained the family profession for many generations. At one time there were five brothers, George, Emmanuel, Theodore, Dimitri and John. From George (1778-1850) descended the Greek Minister, George Baltazzi, who was shot under the government of Gounaris after the Asia Minor disaster. I descend from Theodore (1788-1860). He was an important businessman who was financial advisor to the Sultan and some of the Pashas. For these services the Sultan granted him custom rights on the Galata Bridge. Theodore's wife was from the English family, Sarrell, a very beautiful woman.

There were ten children in all. Theodore's widow appointed Baron Albin Vetsera, a diplomat, twenty-two years older than her, to be a trustee to her children. He invested their entire fortune in Austria and then, in 1864, married one of his wards, the second daughter, Eleni. She was one of the richest girls in Constantinople, so it was advantageous to his career. Not a love match, I have to say. Because of this marriage, all the rest of the Baltazzi siblings moved to Austria. She became the mother of Maria.

One Baltazzi brother, Hector, was an amateur rider, one of the greatest horsemen of his day. He rode to hounds in England, France and Austria, and often rode out with Empress Elisabeth, on her hunting trips to England and Ireland. As a steeplechaser, he won many races. The youngest, Heinrich, was considered a great gentleman, and Arthur Schnitzler drew on his character for the Count in his controversial play, *Reigen* – later made into a well-known film as *La Ronde*. The fourth son, Aristides (1852-1914) was my grandfather. He founded the famous Napajedla stud, the most famous in Austria-Hungary.

My grandparents lived in a beautiful castle built by Fischer von Erlach in the middle of the eighteenth century, inherited by my grandmother. Aristides was also a great horseman, breeding horses at the stud, and a master at promoting good relations with leading breeders and trainers. Every year he invited them to Napajedla, putting on a special train, which left Vienna early in the morning. Breakfast was served on the train and a luncheon of caviar and champagne was laid out in large tents on the lawn near the stud. When everyone was relaxed and happy the horse sales were conducted. After high tea, the guests returned by train with further sumptuous fare for dinner.

My mother, May, was the result of the marriage of Aristides and Countess Stockhau. She was brought up by her father to read English newspapers and discuss them in English. She was a great survivor and in many ways she followed the example of Therese in making the best of difficult situations. This was important as her childhood was overshadowed by the death of her cousin at

Mayerling. She married into the old aristocracy of Austria, which was not easy for her and she was determined to make the best of her life.

A rather unconventional friendship sprang up between her and Count Josef Gizycki, a man who was rather like her uncles, the Baltazzis, although he came from an ancient and very good Polish family and his mother, Ludmilla, came from the distinguished Zamoyski family. Gizyckis' mother was cultivated and had studied the piano under Franz Liszt. She was also a great beauty. Gizycki himself, my mother described as 'handsome, well-built, very intelligent . . . A very literate man, fluent and widely read in many languages.' My mother thought he could have done anything he wanted in life, even been Prime Minister, had he not been so lazy. 'He was an expert on wine, especially burgundy,' my mother remembered. 'He would teach his various women the different tastes of different vintages and years.' She also said that he liked to gamble, but most of all 'women fascinated him and challenged him. And he fascinated women.' Gizycki was interested in having a very good life.

My mother loved Gizycki, I think, and I often wondered if that was the reason that she never re-married later on. He once invited her to Poland. In 1904 he had married the American newspaper heiress, Eleanor ('Cissy') Patterson, from Washington, but, after an unhappy marriage with him which encompassed the kidnapping of their daughter by him, they were divorced. He died when I was about fourteen.

MAYERLING

Maria Vetsera was a first cousin of my mother. As I said, she was the daughter of Eleni Baltazzi, the sister of my grandfather, Aristides Baltazzi. Maria's affair with Crown Prince Rudolph of Austria ended in the famous tragedy at Mayerling. The poor, unstable Crown Prince took her away, as one would now say – for the weekend – and shot her dead at his shooting lodge, Mayerling, not far from Vienna, in January 1889. He then shot himself. The bodies were found there, and it was a terrible tragedy for the Emperor with grave political consequences.

Of course this was not the version that emerged at the time. The first version was that the Crown Prince had fallen victim to an accident, while hunting. The papers said that he had died of an apoplectic stroke. But they soon hinted at murder or suicide and all kinds of rumours filled the air. And then the name of Maria Vetsera began to circulate. I remember Princess Fugger,* a well-known figure in Vienna, who was a friend of my mother's – or perhaps not a friend in reality – telling us that she went round to the Vetsera house and asked to see Maria. She was told that the Baroness was suffering from an inflammation of the throat and so no one was being received.

The Mayerling story was such a strange one. Princess Thurn und Taxis, the friend of Rilke, who housed him for many years at her lovely castle in Trieste, Duino, related a strange tale of foreboding which occurred at Rudolph's christening in 1858. All those gathered round the font held candles. Rudolph's mother handed the baby to his nurse, who was also holding one of these lit candles. The nurse wore her best hat for the ceremony, a black hat with wax cherries around it, such as nurses wore in those days. The candle melted the wax on the hat and some small drops of red wax dropped onto the baby's heart. The nurse was aghast and saw this as a sinister omen. Even if the story is not true, I am surprised that no one used it in the many films about Mayerling, as it is such a haunting image.

Crown Prince Rudolph was a strange man. He had occasionally spoken of his wish to commit suicide in the company of a woman. He once advanced the idea to a prostitute that she might die with him. Understandably she declined. Maria was also rather morbid in her outlook, and once went on record saying that suicide

---

* Princess Fugger (1864-1945). Nora, daughter of Prince Karl zu Hohenlohe-Bartenstein, married 1887, Count Karl Fugger (1861-1925).

should not be condemned. It was well known in Viennese society that the Crown Prince was the victim of illness, which some said was venereal disease. It often was common in military circles, and in those days there existed no cure.

On the fateful night, Maria wrote some letters of farewell to her family and friends. These the Crown Prince put into envelopes addressed to her mother. Then the two deaths occurred.

Many stories have come down in the family about what happened on that January night, one of them a document written by Maria's mother, which Princess Fugger saw. Maria's uncles, Georg Stockhau and Alexander Baltazzi, were sent to the scene by the Emperor to tidy it up and were told by the Emperor never to reveal what they saw. According to Princess Fugger they found Maria with a bullet wound which had entered the left temple and come out again behind the ear. They dressed Maria up after death, seated her in a fiacre with a broomstick attached to her back to keep her upright, and drove her to the neighbouring town of Heiligenkreuz, where she was secretly buried in the cemetery of the Cistercian monastery. What a scene it must have been as they travelled over those roads covered in ice and snow for the burial.

In fact it was so cold that the gravediggers could not do their work until early the following morning. Maria's mother was not allowed to be there – only the two uncles and three policemen, one of whom sent a message to his Chief of Police in Vienna: 'Everything disposed of'. My friend, Count Czernin, said that his father told him what they saw but he would not say what that was. Maria's body remained undisturbed until 1945 when Russian soldiers dug it up, breaking the coffin in quest for jewels.

In my view the court in Vienna behaved in a shocking way, as did the judicial authorities. They were not concerned about Maria – only the posthumous reputation of the heir to the throne. Similarly Maria's mother was accused of trying to promote the relationship, whereas in fact she had hoped for a good union for her daughter. Princess Fugger always denied this, even relating a curious tale about Maria's mother trying to get her married to

Count Fugger, her husband. She would invite him frequently and leave him alone with Maria, who would then sit on his lap and flirt with him. But his sister got to hear about this and intervened. Princess Fugger said that when she heard of Maria's involvement with the Crown Prince, she planned to send her brother, Alexander Baltazzi, to Constantinople with the girl to marry her there because, once she was a married woman, she could do as she wished. It was all most bizarre.

My mother once went to Mayerling to pray there and spoke to the abbess. The nun said to her 'Yes, we all prayed for the *three* souls that died.' This suggests that Maria was expecting a baby.

This tragedy loomed over my family for many years. I was not at all amused when, in about 1983, old Empress Zita told a French journalist (Jean des Cars) that the suicide version was not true and that the Crown Prince and Maria had been murdered as the result of a political plot. She said this could not be disclosed at the time because it would have caused a dangerous threat to the Austrian monarchy. Personally I do not believe this because a political plot would have been less damaging than the morbid suicides. It would have been in the Government's interests to expose such a plot, and they never did so.

The tragedy became the emblem of a crumbling empire. The whole moral structure of Austria was changing and in a way Rudolph represented the new wave. Had Rudolph lived, we might not have seen the break-up of the Austrian Empire, because he was much more liberal and open to new ideas, as is witnessed by his associating with Maria Vetsera in the first place.

The Baltazzis too were moving on a more international scene. They may not have been especially political or deeply cultured, but they were cosmopolitan. They were not hemmed in by the narrow demands of an inter-bred Austrian society. They represented the international flavour of the old Empire.

The salient feature of the Mayerling tragedy was that after it, people began to realise – in Shakespeare's phrase – that 'Something was rotten in the core of Denmark.' The old world was in conflict with the new, and to survive a balance had to be found.

The Baltazzis were all made to suffer on account of Mayerling. This was unfair. Maria's mother knew nothing about the liaison, nor did any of the Baltazzis. Austrian society and the Catholic Church were censorious. In reality they were jealous and suspicious of the rich Baltazzis arriving in their midst. They were much richer than many of the great Austrian families and on account of their success as horse breeders and horsemen were well received, even occasionally by the Emperor, who liked to consult them about equestrian matters.

Just before Mayerling, the Emperor had been about to bestow the title of Count Baltazzi-Stockhau on my grandfather. In the light of it he did not. This was entirely because Maria's mother had been a Baltazzi. It was most unjust. The title was never bestowed. But I do not mind. We had other titles. But I still do not understand why the Baltazzis remained in Austria. Had I been in their situation, I would have moved to England taking horses, stables, treasure and all their surrounding glamour with me. Only one person remained kind to Maria's mother and that was Empress Elisabeth.

My mother had to live with this cloud resting on the family name. It was not her fault, nor anything to do with her directly. She learned to live with gossip. In many ways she was a modern woman, living her life somewhat flamboyantly in contradiction to the will of society.

I too lived some of my early years aware that many disapproved of her and therefore of me also. It strengthened my need to take life in hand, to be courageous and adventurous, to advance into new territories if need be. It created in me a strong determination to survive and to survive well.

Many years later, my great friend Cecilia Sternberg wrote in *The Journey* that I much resembled my cousin Maria, but added: 'Etti would never have died for love of a man.' No, never!

THREE

Early Life 1914-1934

I SPENT MOST of my early life with my mother and younger sister, Sophia, partly in Vienna, but also in the beautiful Italianate castle, Napajedla, in the regions of Moravian Slovakia and Haná, right in the middle of Czechoslovakia. The castle belonged to my Austrian grandmother, Countess Maria (Mitzi) von Stockhau-Baltazzi, the daughter of Friedrich Stockhau (1832-84). She was most amusing – full of life, and knew all the court scandals of the day. As we have seen, she married a rich Greek called Aristides Baltazzi in 1884.

He bought her family out of Napajedla and thus became the owner not only of the castle, which dominated the town, but the fine park which surrounded it, as well as thousands of hectares of arable land, a sawmill, brewery, brickyard and a sugar-house. He reorganised the house, making it a very liveable place. He acquired English pictures and furniture for it, and installed eight bathrooms, a remarkable number for the time. I remember it all very well. My sister and I lived in an English style nursery with an English nurse.

Napajedla was a haven for horses. In 1886 my grandfather founded a stud there to breed English thoroughbreds. The first stallion was *Kisbér*, which Aristides owned jointly with his brother Alexander, and who, as I already said, won the Epsom Derby in 1876. The Baltazzi brothers were well known in Vienna and internationally. They were racing friends of King Edward VII. *Kisbér* was the best stallion at the stud, which soon produced a band of thoroughbred horses which was renowned all over Europe. Every year, in June, a special train would bring fifty friends of the family to the stud from Vienna. There would be a huge dinner, served in giant tents set up on the lawn, and a party. Then they would auction fifty yearlings sired by the great stallions.

It was there, at Napajedla, that I learned to love horses and to understand them. The fields surrounding the castle were full of magnificent thoroughbreds. There were Lipizzaners from the Spanish Riding School in Vienna to pull the carriages. I spent hours playing with them and riding them and these were some of my happiest childhood memories. My interest was more than the usual equestrian interests of a youngster. I studied the ancestry of the horses and their stud records. I developed a rapport with the stallions, mares and foals, and learned their ways. My friend, Cecilia Sternberg, observed me in the paddock and wrote of this early interest of mine: 'I have never seen anything more beautiful than this small girl running beside the huge white stallions as they trotted and cantered to her orders. The virgin and the unicorn.'

Cecilia also described me at the castle: 'She was small and thin, yet proportionally perfectly shaped and rounded. She wore a pink cotton dress, her hair was brown, long and somewhat tousled and her pointed childish face enchantingly pretty.' I quite like this description.

My parents did not enjoy a happy marriage. My grandmother never liked my father, saying of him: 'He is quite nice – but what a bore!' My parents were divorced in 1918, when I was four. My father did not play a part in my upbringing. He was very nice, very Austrian – and charming. After the divorce I do not think we ever saw him again. He died in December 1933, before I was twenty.

Nor did my mother and grandmother get on well together. So my mother took us travelling with her. We moved restlessly through Europe, moving from one family castle to another, or to resorts such as Monte Carlo, where my mother loved to gamble. Here, close to where I live now, we watched the men shooting pigeons below the great edifice of the Casino. Or we went to Roquebrune where my mother had a house.

Sometimes we children were sent up to the mountains to Peraclava. At other times we went to Rome, where my mother, herself an expert horsewoman, liked to hunt in the Campagna Romana. In those days you could gallop round it, and she would jump the Stationata on the outskirts of Rome.

My sister and I inherited the love of animals from our grandfather. He loved animals so much that he never gave a shooting party for his friends. This rather outraged them! He left any shooting to his gamekeepers. He preferred the breeding of horses and was a leading member of the Vienna Jockey Club. We children made friends with the family horses, and spent a lot of time with the children of my grandfather's household – of the administrator, the gardeners and the coachmen – but much of my childhood was solitary. I lacked the traditional network of friends of the same age with whom to play, which should have been normal in the kind of family that I came from. So I have to say there was no warm and stable atmosphere in which to develop. My companions were my mother, my sister and a French governess. There were few family reunions or parties.

When I was ten, I nearly died. We were then living in Berlin and I fell ill with tuberculosis. My mother heard the nurse coughing and of course I immediately caught it. I can still remember the nurse saying: 'Take the candles. This child is going to die.' I was sent to the Waltzaner Sanatorium in Davos, later made famous in Thomas Mann's novel, *The Magic Mountain*. Like the hero, Hans Castorp, I was taken by train along the narrow pass, where water roared in the abyss, through the rocks and past the dark fir-trees pointing up towards a stone-grey sky. Vista after vista opened before me as I made my way up into the mountains. I was collected by a liveried figure and conveyed to a plateau near wooded slopes where the clinic stood.

This was to be my home for the next two years. The clinic had a garden with flowerbeds, gravel paths and even a grotto. In the hall there were reclining chairs and the roof could be opened so that the patients could take the fresh air. All kinds of patients were here, some of them rather mysterious, melancholy figures for whom the trials of life had proved too great. There were endless figures lying listlessly on balconies. Cures were slow in those days. There were no antibiotics and so the treatment was necessarily long and had to take its time. I spent most of my time either lying in bed or recuperating on a *chaise longue* on the balcony. Friends of my mother came to see me and we had meals together in the clinic's restaurant just off the main hall.

The days here seemed unending to a child, surrounded on all sides by illness, discussions of maladies and temperatures, hoped for cures, relapses and sometimes even death.

When I was better, I was educated by a governess, German being my first language and English my second. After 1926 we travelled in Italy and France. From 1929 to the spring of 1931, we received an allowance of 12,000 to 15,000 francs a month from my grandmother.

After her divorce, my mother preferred places where the life was rather international. She did not like Vienna which she thought of as rather a gossipy place, very strict, and disapproving of divorce. She was never good-looking but she had a lot of charm. And she had a succession of lovers. Some of them I didn't quite approve of. But she never remarried.

Maybe this restlessness infected me too. In my life I have married six times. I am proud to say that each of the husbands was absolutely different. Life changed completely with each marriage but this has never worried me. One of the secrets for a happy marriage is that the wife should become absorbed in those things that fascinate her husband. My daughter Bunny says of me: 'I really think that if my mother married a man who collected butterflies, she would suddenly develop an interest in butterflies!' I like living for somebody. You learn so much. I think a woman must be married. I have also been engaged a number of times without getting married.

I was still very young – about sixteen – when my mother lost the security that had allowed us to live the particular life she enjoyed.

My grandmother was the victim of a terrible confidence trick, which ruined her and left us all in a sorry situation.

Some time in 1929 or 1930 Herr Gerscher, the administrator at Napajedla, told my grandmother that oil had been found on the estate. I was in the drawing room with my sister when he came in with this news. His team had been drilling a new well in the park, hoping for water and had found oil. To prove this he presented my grandmother with a small bottle of oil. This she opened, sniffed it approvingly and passed it round to the other tea guests. Everyone was excited with the exception of Herr Bata, founder of the Bata shoe industry. He took the bottle into his callous hands – callous from his hard work as a shoemaker in his youth. He too sniffed and sniffed again. Then he shook his head and looked at my grandmother. But she was not to be deterred. Nothing would dissuade her from being thrilled at identifying oil on the estate.

She conceived the crazy idea of instigating an expensive digging programme on the estate. Gerscher came forward with an elaborate plan which of course required substantial funds. My grandmother had considerable capital. She decided not to involve a major oil company. She would finance the operation. Gerscher was secretly delighted. He was even more pleased when she began to provide him with the funds he needed for the operation. Expensive modern outfits were ordered from Germany and the work proceeded.

In fact he tricked her. Every week he would arrive with another little bottle, claiming to have found it on the estate, and week after week, my grandmother would hand over more money. But no oil was found and the costs were such that in due course the capital ran out. The bankers refused any further credit. My grandmother was furious. Up till then she had treated bankers as poor money lenders and they had always been most respectful to her. But not any more.

In the spring of 1931 the trusted administrator disappeared, taking his family with him. The banks closed in. Old Bata shook his head in horror, and my grandmother fled the journalists, taking refuge with relatives in a nearby castle. Then she settled for a year in Menton.

Unaware of these developments, my mother, then in Monte Carlo, became alarmed when her allowance mysteriously ceased. It was a worry since she was the heir to the entire estate. Assuming there was some misunderstanding, she took a train, bringing my sister and me with her, but she found no one at the station to meet us. The man who drove us to the castle gave his version of the preceding drama, and told her that the old Countess had fled. My mother arrived to see removal men taking the furniture away. We children stood there crying our eyes out. We even saw our toys going – Sophia noticing a lovely tortoise toiletry set initialled with a crown, the gift of an aunt, disappearing with these objects. My mother visited the banks in Bruenn. The full story was spread out to her horror.

My mother tried to run the estate and for a time was able to send my grandmother an allowance. But in the spring of 1932 the estate was sorely pressed by creditors, and was placed under a compulsory administration by order of the courts. Napajedla was sold – the castle, the surrounding lands and all its treasures. Today it is the National Stud of the Czech Republic. After that my mother had very little money.

Things looked desperate and then all of a sudden an admirer came into my life, so rich that he was presently offering to save Napajedla. In May 1932 I went to Budapest for a time, and then in June I went to stay with my mother's friend, Princess Fugger. While I was in Vienna my aunt, Charlotte Wurmbrand, handed me a letter from a young man. This man had seen me in Budapest and wished to see me again. So I went to Salzburg to meet him. Two days later I was engaged to Baron Charles Buxhoeveden.

I was seventeen years old, very pretty and I had great success. I have mentioned my sudden engagement. But Charlie Buxhoeveden was not the love of my life. I had fallen madly in love with a young man called Count Vladschi Mittrovsky. He was a man about town in Viennese society the year that I 'came out',

43

and he was heir to a neighbouring property in Czechoslovakia, one of the largest and most beautiful castles in Moravia. He was a great shot and accompanied me to many shooting parties. He was even a little deaf from shooting. Perhaps he drank a little too much, but I did not mind.

While Vladschi was dithering, there occurred the engagement with Charlie Buxhoeveden. Charlie was good-looking, elegant and full of life. As an international young sportsman he divided his time between St Moritz, the South of France and at one time Napajedla. He was a Russian of Baltic origin, and had inherited a considerable fortune in Germany from his mother who was a Siemens. Charlie was without a home and searching for somewhere to settle and for a wife. He proposed to me at the height of the Napajedla troubles, even offering to save the estate. We became engaged. A rich marriage – it sounded the solution to all our problems. We did not know where Charlie lived other than that he was based in Berlin, but we did know he had an annual income of 300,000 gold marks.

My mother borrowed money (4,000 crowns) and came to Salzburg. The engagement was announced in the papers, and the date for the wedding set, some time in November 1932. My mother talked to Charlie about her lack of resources. In Vienna we stayed at the Hotel Sacher, the managers deferring the bill until funds became available after my marriage. The hotel agreed to this knowing that my wedding would be celebrated in great style.

A month later I realised that I was far too much in love with Vladschi to see this through. This time it was I who hesitated. Would I really be happy with Charlie, strong, Russian and German? Could I not still win Vladschi round? I was still seeing Vladschi occasionally by stealth. Financial matters did not concern me as I was too young to understand the implications. Besides, Vladschi would one day inherit a fine estate in Moravia. At this time Napajedla disappeared. Eventually my hesitation became too desperate. Charlie and I both agreed that it would be best to break off the engagement.

My mother was then in serious trouble. She was arrested over her unpaid hotel bill and bills for expensive clothes bought but not paid for. On 10 July 1933 I testified at the Criminal District Court in Vienna stating that we had no money, owned nothing but owed much. All these debts had been incurred in anticipation of my marriage. Charlie paid my mother 45,000 schillings in indemnity.

Then I was briefly engaged to Vladschi in August 1933. He loved me, he was charming but he was weak. Gradually he fell more and more under the influence of his family. They wanted him to make a rich marriage and sadly I was no longer rich. They wanted a dowry that mine could not provide. Cecilia Sternberg wrote that all Vladschi had was his allowance, three guns, a lot of suits and a sports car, being dependent, in all other respects on his father. Certainly I had very little, though I dressed well in clothes sent to me from Paris by my mother, and described by Cecilia as 'the latest Paris *jeune fille* fashion'. My family were also against this marriage, because Vladschi suffered from a rare blood disease. So this engagement was also broken off. I felt deceived and deserted. Meanwhile, Charlie, tired of my hesitations, had left Vienna.

There was also a Senor Ferrera, an Argentinian millionaire, to whom I was briefly engaged. His name came up later when I was in trouble in America.

Old Princess Fugger said to my mother: 'Well, my dear May, what are you going to do with your daughters now? They will have to work!'

I was there and I heard my mother replying: 'My daughters will make very rich marriages.' The idea of her daughters working filled her with horror.

The story of suitors was not over. At that moment a very rich young American heir arrived in Vienna. He was called Clendenin Ryan.

I had met my first husband.

FOUR

Husband 1
Mr Clendenin Ryan Jr., 1934-1935

Clendenin James Ryan Jr. (1905-1957)
Born in New York 1905.
Married (1) 1934, Countess Etti Wurmbrand. Divorced 1935.
Married (2) 1937, Jean Harder. Two sons, two daughters.
(She married secondly, 1969, William Shields, Jr. (d 1979),
and died 1991).
Died New York 12 September 1957.

CLENDENIN RYAN arrived in Vienna and I thought he was quite good looking, strongly Catholic but with a slight inclination to melancholy. He said he needed someone to cheer him up. He was more specific – an aristocratic girl from a good Catholic family. I was both those things. As Vladschi was clearly not going to make up his mind, I had some dates with Clen. On the third date he proposed and I accepted.

My mother approved of this. She was happy with the solution that I should cross the Atlantic and marry an American boy – a rich husband in that new world where values were so different from ours. To give me a good start she ordered me a sumptuous trousseau from Braun's in Vienna, all the pieces embroidered with the cipher and coronet of our family. She paid the couturiers with cheques and she paid my fare to New York with another cheque. The trousseau was sent over to Clen's family address in New York. My mother did not seem overly concerned that she did not have funds to cover this. She said that a friend called Tommy

Esterházy (later to be my third husband) owed her some money, which would cover this. He was to pay her on the day I sailed.

Clen came from the rich New York Catholic family of Ryans and was a cousin of John Barry Ryan, whose wife 'Nin' was at the centre of cultural life in New York and keenly involved with the opera there. The Ryans came originally from a small farm in Nelson, Virginia. Clen's grandfather, Thomas Fortune Ryan, left there as a young man and made his way to Baltimore. He was a penniless orphan with a good future ahead of him. He walked the streets until being taken on as a messenger boy in a dry goods firm run by John S. Barry. He married the boss's daughter and moved to New York. He soon became a partner in his own firm with his own seat on the New York Stock Exchange. The fortune was established through a hugely successful web of railroads, coal companies, tobacco, life insurance and later his reorganisation of the Belgian Congo diamond fields. On his death he left an estate worth $135 million. Clen himself received part of a trust fund judged to be worth more than $141 million.

It was a relief and joy to be able to distance myself from my sorrows over Vladschi. My great friend, Marjorie Oelrichs, accompanied me on the voyage to New York at the end of 1933. Marjorie was a lovely girl, wholly American but completely at ease in any European country. She had beautiful waxen skin and eyebrows like butterflies' antennae. She loved to laugh, but she could be reproachful too. 'Now really,' she would say as a firm but gentle reproof. Everyone loved her, and Anita Loos described her affectionately as 'soft, plump and beautiful, she was a high-society version of Mae West. Her voice was a sexy wheeze but, contrary to Mae, her brain was like a bag of popcorn.' Her life took on a number of unconventional turns. She upset her family by posing for Lucky Strike advertisements. I read that she seduced Cecil Beaton when he went to America, giving him his first experiences with a woman. She was so kind. Then in 1935 she took the unconventional path of marrying the bandleader, Eddy Duchin. In August 1937, she died tragically and unnecessarily, giving birth to her son Peter, himself a top society bandleader and pianist without whose presence no great party is complete anywhere in the world.

Marjorie was the perfect companion for a love-lorn girl on her way to the United States. The crossing was rough and I still recall the hours of seasickness in my cabin. Eventually, after what seemed a never-to-end sea voyage, we arrived in Manhattan on 13 December 1933 where I was greeted by Clen on the boat, conducted to a special barge covered in roses, escorted into his Rolls Royce, again half-hidden with roses, and driven to the house where I was to stay. Crowds of photographers took hundreds of photographs of me as I disembarked from the ship. I waved at them graciously as I had seen photographs of other women doing when confronted with the flash cameras.

Hardly had I arrived at the house when I was given a telegram sent by Princess Fugger, informing me that my mother had been arrested and was in gaol! Imagine my shock! I discovered that Tommy had not paid his debt, that the cheques had not been honoured and that Braun's had informed the police. So my mother was arrested and taken away, leaving my 14-year-old sister behind her. Sophia used her initiative and contacted the lawyer who had handled the Napajedla crisis. He contacted Tommy's Jewish *homme d'affaires*, a rather more worldly figure than Tommy. He settled things and the lawyer and my sister then collected my mother and drove her from the prison in a smart fiacre to the Hotel Sacher, where Wolly Seybel, a man about town and friend of my mother's, gave her a sumptuous luncheon party.

From that day on my mother never used cheques. She always paid by cash, and she came to consider all bankers to be crooks. I do not believe she ever had a bank account after that. The incident further distanced her from the Austrian aristocracy, not one of whom had moved a finger to help her. This was another reason why she was happy that I was marrying an American in the new world.

I went to stay with some cousins, Prince Chlodwig Hohenlohe-Schillingsfürst and his wife Mabel Taylor, the former Mrs Gifford Cochran, a lady from Philadelphia, eleven years his senior. They spent part of their year at Alt-Aussee, Styria, in Austria and when in America, they lived at the River House, 435 East 52nd Street, where I lived with them during my first brief, but not un-dramatic sojourn amongst the skyscrapers of New York.

New York was a city of cocktail parties. Clen and I went from one party to the next. Clen was then secretary to the famous Mayor of New York, Fiorello H. La Guardia, and had been an active Republican for some years. With some friends he had founded a group called the Fusioneers, who helped to get Mayor La Guardia elected. La Guardia was quite attractive and pleasant, but he had character defects and he was very much against us Europeans. Clen tried to divine my every wish. Each day he sent me flowers, the scent of which almost suffocated me. His family were kind, but those devoutly Catholic sisters of his almost suffocated me too.

I relished the American way of life. The Americans do not complicate life as we do in Europe. I suppose I was thought unusual as the Americans do not see many Austrians in New York. Clen was kind to me. He thought he did not spoil me enough. He spoiled me too much. But there was one thing he could not give me. He could not give me Valdschi, with all his charm and weaknesses, and his indecision. I yearned to return to Europe and to Vladschi.

But it was not to be. Our engagement was announced in the newspapers on 12 February 1934. The entertaining increased. One rather startling party was a beautiful pre-nuptial ball given by the legendary (and somewhat predatory) beauty, Mona Harrison Williams (later Countess Bismarck). She was absolutely fantastic and one of the most beautiful women I ever saw with her green eyes and red hair. At this party everything matched. Her house at 1130 Fifth Avenue was filled with pink carnations from their house in Long Island and her dress was the same colour as the carnations. Mona herself wore a wonderful emerald necklace and earrings that matched her lovely eyes. She was very pretty. I was a bit surprised when she followed me into a room and closed the door behind her. I had to escape. I did not know she was like that.

Clendenin Ryan became my first husband at a huge wedding at St Patrick's Cathedral on 20 February. For the ceremony I wore a gown of white duchess satin with a long train and a *fichu* of rose-point lace. The wedding in the Lady Chapel of the cathedral was attended by Mayor La Guardia and the best man was Howard Cushing. Yet in my heart I knew I was destined for unhappiness. Before I left home I told Prince Hohenlohe that I could not go through with the wedding because I loved only Vladschi, but it was too late. I arrived at the cathedral in tears, on the arm of Prince Hohenlohe. The papers were full of reports of the 'sweet bride' and how I had won all American hearts. I got particularly sick of that description. Wherever we went, we were followed by press photographers. That is how it was with society figures in those days.

After our honeymoon in the South, we set up home in New York. My first marriage proved short-lived. I soon discovered that my husband was an alcoholic. About once a month, he got drunk, which was frightening for a young girl. He was terrible when he got drunk. If it had not been for that, probably I could have been happy with him. My worries over his drinking sharpened my mind, and I realised that I could not escape my love for Vladschi so easily.

I stayed in touch with Vladschi secretly and this unfortunately got me into trouble. I wrote him letters and one time I sent him a telegram assuring him that I still loved him. I did not realise that a copy would be sent to me. Worse than that, it was sent to my mother-in-law by mistake. She wasted no time in alerting her son.

One day I went to Cartier's and chose a beautiful wrist watch – a Santos model, on the back of which I asked them to engrave the words: 'Valdschi – every hour I think of you with love.' Obviously

I had no money of my own, so I made them charge this to Clen's account. It never occurred to me that he would notice, since he sent me so many jewels that way. Maybe he would not have done, but the man from Cartier's brought the watch to our house before I had the chance to go in and collect it.

It was awful. Clen opened the package rather excitedly. He was deeply touched that I should have gone to the trouble to get him such a beautiful gift. He was just putting it on his wrist when he turned it round and spotted the inscription.

'What's that? Vladschi?' he said. 'I'm not Vladschi. Cartier's must have made a mistake. They have sent the wrong watch. A firm like Cartier's should not make a mistake like that.' He rang the shop and half an hour later one of the directors arrived, somewhat out of breath to explain himself. He said there had been no mistake. Mrs Ryan had ordered that inscription.

Clen went pale and when we were alone, he asked me: 'Who the hell is Vladschi?'

'That is the man I love,' I replied rather dramatically. Clen rose, opened the window, and threw the watch out into the street. Some lucky passer-by no doubt picked it up. After that Clen never mentioned the incident again, but I knew he was deeply hurt. Men do not like being made fools of.

This was a serious hitch. Though Clen did not speak of it again, I became conscious that every time I went out shopping alone, I was followed by a sinister looking man in a raincoat with a black hat drawn across his face. He was clearly a detective and he was not there to protect me but to spy on me. I asked Clen about the man, but he did not answer.

The situation deteriorated. There was a drama when some jewels I had been given were stolen from my bag at the Metropolitan Opera House, when I was preparing to take part in the Opera Ball. The press said they were worth a thousand dollars. After two months Clen and I separated. I moved to the Pierre at the expense of the Ryan family and my husband put out a statement, saying: 'I am not living with her and I am not going back there.'

I suddenly found myself trailed by five detectives wherever I went. I felt lost. I remembered meeting A.C. Blumenthal, the Broadway producer, often known as 'Blumie'. So I called him and asked him what I should do. He recommended his attorney, Nathan Burkan, of 1450 Broadway, a famous Jewish lawyer who specialised in the theatre and had represented people like Mae West, Charlie Chaplin and Al Jolson. Blumie said to me: 'He's tops! I know he can straighten you out.' The press claimed he paid the fees too. What actually happened was that Nat Burkan called me up and said that he hated my husband and that he would do anything to help me get a settlement. He loathed Clen so much that he would represent me without a fee. This was just as well. I gather that although he got Mae West acquitted when her play, *Sex*, was raided in New York in 1927, his legal fees bankrupted her!

Nat was a great asset. When I was staying at Great Neck with him, we found hired sleuths concealed in the shrubbery around the property. If I went to the hairdresser's they were there, and when I went out in the evening, I found them appropriately clad in evening dress. When addressing the press one day, Nat said: 'I'm going to the Hotel Pierre to take the Countess and five detectives to luncheon.' Nat attacked Clen's attorney, George W. Whiteside about these sleuths, and he admitted that they had been engaged. He said that they were also 'seeking valuable information in Vienna, Paris, Monte Carlo and other such places.'

None of this happened quietly. In May the papers announced that Clen was filing an annulment suit against me. He accused me of 'conspiring with unidentified persons to obtain large sums of money from the Ryan family, with having exaggerated the wealth of her own family and with having rushed him into marriage.' I was also accused of what he called 'misconduct before marriage.' He said that I had been plotting the marriage since 1 November 1933. The way he had been rushed into marriage was that I had apparently told him my mother was opposed to the idea of my marrying an American and wanted a noble European match for me. Therefore the marriage had to be fixed very quickly.

Nat Burkan demanded a quick resolution of all this, announcing that I was stranded in a strange city, admittedly in an hotel, but without five cents to my name. As I was under age, I had to have a guardian appointed – the former Assistant District Attorney, Rose Rothenburg. In Nat's office, I was referred to as 'the Infant'. The judge said: 'I want no anger. I would like to straighten this matter without a brown taste in everybody's mouth.'

There were daily headlines proclaiming: 'RYAN CHARGES PLOT LED TO MARRIAGE' – accusing my mother and myself as being embroiled in a plot to lay our hands on Clendenin's fortune! They said that I was trying to obtain a share of Thomas Fortune Ryan's inheritance and that my husband left me as soon as he learnt of my conspiracy. All in all, twenty-three charges were put out against me, all of which I refuted. The publicity was terrible. Dreadful rhymes even appeared in the papers:

'R stands for Ryan –
The Countess unthawed –
Is charged by Clendenin
For being a fraud.'
The Divorcees' Alphabet.

I still went out in New York, the press describing my various outfits and engagements. I created a stir by wearing a white evening dress with a bow at a high neckline and a jaunty peplum jutting out *à la Schiaparelli*. I told them I was doing a screen test for MGM, just for fun. I was accused of being dated by A.C. Blumenthal. He had just produced *Music in the Air* and *Eight Bells* on Broadway, was sensationally rich and in the middle of a rather here-and–there marriage to the Broadway star, Peggy Fears. Blumie kindly took me out to dinner a few times and was of course spotted by the detectives. When challenged by the press, he said: 'Hell! Can't a guy take a gal out without being nuts about her? She's just a kid jammed up in a strange land and I feel sorry for her.' But a little later he rather over-egged it by saying: 'Now, you're not going to print all that Ryan stuff, are you? All right, go ahead. Tell the world I've been a mug for women all my life.'

I went to El Morocco with Erskine Gwynne, whose mother was a Vanderbilt, and who had recently been divorced from his wife, 'Foxy', who later married Lord Sefton. I dined at the Paradise. I was not hiding in my hotel room in those difficult months. One evening I caused wry laughter when I happened to enter the restaurant of the Pierre, just as a wedding party was taking place and the Lohengrin wedding march was being played. The press described my arrival as follows: 'With a sphinx-like face Mrs Ryan took her place at a table and was later joined by an escort.' I was photographed by the wonderful Baron de Meyer in a Viennese morning jacket.

Clen's attorneys continued to attack me, accusing me of going to expensive restaurants and running up a big bill at the Pierre. A writ was served on my mother. They found her at the Hotel Meisel and Schadn in Vienna.

Presently the situation became unbearable in New York so I did the only thing a girl can do in a situation like this. I sailed away. Just before I left I ordered another Santos watch from Cartier's with the same inscription and paid for it with cash. I spent my last dollars on that watch, and Cartier's were delighted to provide it as it showed that the wife of their celebrated client, Clendenin Ryan, was no longer angry with them.

On 18 June I left America on board the North German Lloyd liner, *Europa*, in another swarm of press photographs, all of which showed me in a pretty shell-pink chiffon cocktail dress with pink roses encircling my neck, the kind of outfit traditionally worn on board in those days. I told the journalists that I would be back in September to answer my husband's charges. One of them was especially cheeky with his questions. He asked me: 'Seriously now, when you told Mr Ryan about those other eggs – Count Mittrovsky, Baron Buxhoeveden and Senor Ferrera, you weren't taking him for a buggy ride, were you?'

I replied: 'A buggy ride? Oh I understand. Certainly not. Those what you calls eggs are all right. One of them is in Africa right now.'

'Which one?'

'It doesn't matter. Where is that champagne?'

In the end I had to quote back to these men: 'You have a funny expression here in America. I believe it goes like this – Nothing is sure except death and rent day.'

I was happy to leave behind me the unwelcome publicity and legal tangles. Hardly was I aboard than I noticed that the detective in the rain coat was also on board, only now he had exchanged his black hat for a black sporting cap. I waved at him but he looked away. There were four other men just like him also on the voyage. They were nicknamed 'The five daddies!' At first I found this quite amusing as it was a new feeling being watched so intensely. In fact I told the journalists: 'I was pleased to know they were coming. I have got used to them. I should have been miserable and lonely without them. We are not hiring any detectives to watch Mr Ryan's detectives, however, because then he would have to hire more to watch ours, and then – they would sink the ship.'

I had left the Ryan jewels in New York, and Clen had promised to put them in the safe for me. After all, I might just return. But being watched by those detectives every time I went into dinner or back to my cabin, I became outraged and decided that I would never return to Clen. On board the ship, I went to the shop and bought an album. I spent much of the voyage sticking in the intensely disagreeable articles about me, which I thought might amuse – and astonish – my Austrian friends on my return home.

The *Europa* docked at Cherbourg. I was furious when I discovered I was still being followed – this time all the way to Paris by two men with peculiar moustaches. I threw something of a tantrum. It was not an easy time. I knew my mother would not be pleased at my desertion of Clendenin Ryan, but I was determined not to sacrifice myself any more. There were other

55

possible husbands in the world, and I had not lost my optimism. I arrived back in Europe and headed to my mother in Vienna. On disembarking, I was quoted as saying: 'It is so easy to throw mud at a woman who has no chance to defend herself. I returned from America without a penny in my pocket, so you can see what a skilful gold-digger I am!'

In July I went to Vienna, while I spent August with my mother at the Hotel de l'Europe in Salzburg in order to escape surveillance. I acquired a Russian wolfhound which followed me around like the detectives. I did give one interview in which I said I would be prepared to return to my husband but not to my mother-in-law. Clen was too much under her influence.

I never saw Clen again. I never asked for anything. I should have asked for a substantial sum of money. It was really too stupid.

The marriage annulment case was heard in the New York Courts in August 1934, Justice Salvatore A. Cotillo (the first Italian ever elected to the New York State Assembly) going so far as to describe it as 'an example of international gold-digging by so-called nobility.' My marriage was described as 'a kissless marriage' followed by an 'ice-box honeymoon.' They said I had locked the bedroom door on my husband.

A divorce was granted on the grounds that I had (1) misrepresented my social position, wealth, upbringing; (2) been bought off in my two previous engagements; (3) married Clendenin with the purpose of dissolving the marriage, and obtaining a settlement enabling me to return to a previous love – Vladschi.

The press thought that Cotillo had Barbara Hutton's recent marriage to Alexis Mdvani in mind when he summed up:

'The records of our courts and the public press affords ample proof that alliances between Americans of either sex with titled foreigners are fraught with peril and almost invariably end in disaster. . . . It is not a source of satisfaction to see our marriage institution and our courts made mere incidents to the purchase and sale of foreign titles . . . '.

'[Ryan] obviously was unaccustomed to dealing with the workings of a shrewd and cunning European mind and doubtless was attracted by the glamour of foreign titles and his contact with Continental nobility. In permitting himself to be deceived by the sham of class or caste based upon the accident of birth, [he] lost sight of the fact that his own country is firmly grounded in principles opposed to divine rights of titled personages.'

Hot on its heels came another law case in which my former maid, Dorothy Pawlowsky sued Clen's chief investigator, John G. Broady in the Supreme Court, saying that he had made love to her and promised her marriage in order to obtain evidence against me.

I did not get my first marriage annulled in Rome until years later, when the papers had to be served in the Vatican. That is why when I married my sixth husband, we were only married civilly, but after the annulment we could get married again in church.

As for Clen, in 1937 he remarried to a Miss Jean Harder of New York. Ten years his junior, she was a socially registered Junior Leaguer who served on the staff of the Civic Information Bureau, which helped La Guardia get re-elected. I gather he bought the Panther Ledge Estate in New Jersey from the Sanfords, and reared Angus cattle there. They say he kept alligators in the basement of his house and fed them with live chicken. They had five children.

Evidently Clen took to engaging in political crusades against crime and corruption in public life. Having got a taste for employing private investigators to follow me, he employed many more to look into public wrong doings, and often testified personally before grand juries. Ironically, he denounced corruption in the administration of Mayor William O'Dwyer after the Second World War – I say ironically because Bill O'Dwyer and I crossed paths in South America at about that time.

Clen hoped to get the Democratic nomination as Governor in New Jersey in 1953, but that did not work out. In 1957 he was being sued for not paying a promised $125,000 towards the financing of a magazine called *Know the Facts*. That September he was about to go to Washington for the case. His lawyer, Michael Graney, arrived at his house 32 East 70th Street, to accompany him to the court, and Clen beckoned him into his study. Then he excused himself and went to the bathroom.

Next thing the lawyer heard was a shot, and on rushing in, found Clen in a pool of blood, a shot wound through the head, and a .45 calibre automatic pistol and three suicide notes lying in the basin. He died. Apparently he had been suffering from severe mental depression for some time.

Clen was following in his father's footsteps – very literally. His father, Clendenin Ryan, Sr, had gassed himself to death in the same house in August 1939.

FIVE

Husband 2
Count Pali Pálffy, 1935-1937

Count Franz Paul Rudolf Maria Joseph Pálffy (1890-1968)
Born Vienna, 12 February 1890.
Married (1) 1915, Franziska-Romana, Grafin Esterházy von
Galantha (1890-1935). Divorced 1920. (She married secondly,
1924, Prince Bela Odescalchi – 1890-1954).
Married (2) 1922, Dorothy Deacon (1891-1960), formerly wife
of Prince Anton Albrycht Radziwill. Divorced 1928.
One son, one daughter.
Married (3) 1928, Eleanor Greene Roelker (1890-1952),
formerly wife of Harrison Tweed. Divorced 1934.
Married (4) 1935, Countess Etti Wurmbrand. Divorced 1937.
Married (5) 1938, Louise de Vilmorin (1902-69).
Divorced 1943.
Married (6) 1946, Edith Hoch (b.1923). Divorced 1949.
Married (7) 1951, Marie-Theresa, Grafin zu Herberstein-
Proskaw (b.1928). Divorced 1956. (She married secondly, Franz
Gf. Zichy de Zich et Vasukoe).
Married (8) 1956, Carin Braun von Stumm (b.1923). One son.
Died Munich, 11 October 1968.

IHAD CABLED Vladschi from the boat to alert him to my return
and asked him to wait for me in Vienna. It was wonderful to see
him on the station with a large bunch of red roses. I gave him the
lovely watch and told him of my misadventures. He thought these
very funny. We were soon dining and dancing every night, but

unfortunately he remained as vague as ever about the idea of marrying. The marriage question had been made more difficult, of course. Not only was I no longer an heiress, but I had been married in church. I needed a divorce and an annulment. Then Vladschi began to drink more heavily. I hate to confess that I became rather bored. I think we were not the same youngsters as we had been such a short time before. By July it was pretty much over for good.

There were other things to worry about. In October there was the final annulment hearing in New York, to which I did not return. In the same month my mother was brought to court in Vienna and given a two-year suspended sentence and put on probation on account of her debts. She then went to the gaming tables of the State Gambling Casino at Baden, about fifteen miles south of the city, to try to convert a $40 stake into $2,000. My mother was very angry about what had happened to me. When the press located her, she said: 'Of course we have nothing against Americans in general. We were disappointed, yes, but maybe there are also chivalrous and understanding men of that species.'

In the same October I arrived in Vienna with Cecilia Sternberg, and as though I had not suffered enough bad publicity, found myself questioned when $6,000 worth of jewels were stolen from the Hotel Sacher, where the Sternbergs, my mother and I were all staying. I was never a suspect, but understandably I became most upset (the press said 'hysterical') when questioned at police headquarters.

One evening Vladschi and I went to one of the most famous nightclubs in Vienna, where normally we were greeted with great respect and a lot of attention. On this evening nobody seemed to notice us at all. My favourite song – 'Smoke gets in your eyes' – was being played and I realised that the centre of attention was further in the club. In a corner of the club, a part lit only by candles there stood a huge man, surrounded by an Hungarian gypsy band. He was singing in a deep baritone voice those marvellous Hungarian songs that bring tears to the eyes, or make a shudder go up your spine.

He was just finishing another favourite song – 'Krasznahorka' – a tragic love story about a haunted castle in Northern Hungary when suddenly I saw him advancing towards me, followed by his troupe of gypsies, still playing. Then I recognised him as Pali Pálffy, an Hungarian Count and a distant cousin of ours (as was his first wife) and a man famous for his good looks and charm as a 'lady killer'. Few women could resist him and when he sang, it was Heaven on Earth. He had brought his Tziganes, or gypsy band, to Vienna from his estate, Pudmerice, in Slovakia. Sometimes he took them with him to St Moritz to enliven his dinners.

Standing close, his big blue eyes looked down at me. He was a magician so far as women were concerned, very fascinating. He did not leave my side for a moment that night. Next day he met my mother at lunch at the Hotel Sacher. He told her: 'Etti is a darling. I love her and I am going to marry her.'

My mother, aware that he had just divorced his third wife, told him: 'But you are much too old for her. You are forty! You could be her father!'

'Perhaps I could adopt her?' he enquired with a twinkle.

He was probably lonely. We thought we might have a good time together. It was not a serious love affair at first, but Pali was great fun to be with. He was charming and good looking. When we got engaged he liked to tell people that he had held me on his knee when I was a baby.

He stood up for me in my public travails with the press, telling them: 'Look here! The whole world is out to crush this young girl because she preferred to leave that dollar prince without taking a penny from him, rather than stay with him just to become a rich woman. I am about to marry the finest, loveliest woman on earth. This lady deserves a husband who understands her.' So sweet! In turn I said I was looking forward to being 'a quiet little countess'.

Pali's past was romantic. When he was a small baby, his mother had jumped out of the window of the family castle, Pudmerice, with Pali in her arms, and ran off with a fabulously rich Italian lover, Dentice di Frasso, whom she subsequently married. The incident caused a sensation at the time.

Men such as Pali no longer exist. Though he never had much money, he had many servants. They all adored him. When he left on the Orient Express for a journey, they were all lined up to see him off. He lived a fabulous life, approaching everything he did with great charm. He was immaculately dressed, his suits coming from the best London tailor of the day, and his shoes from Lobb. He was at home wherever he was in the world.

Pali was born in Vienna in 1890. He descended from an old Austro-Hungarian family, who traced their origins back to the Counts of Wiesselburg in 1330. The name Pálffy means 'Pauli filius' or son of Paul. They became Barons of Hungary in 1581, Counts of the Holy Roman Empire in 1599 and finally Counts Pálffy d'Erdöd in Vienna in 1634.

In the 1970s, Pali's son, Johnnie, used to announce: 'My father was married eight times – once to my mother!' He certainly had eight wives and I think I knew all of them. There were many jokes about this. It was said that he created more Countesses than the Pope. Then his friends asked him why he married so often. If he was in a polite mood, he replied: 'I felt sorry for them.' If not, then he joked: 'I don't want to have to go to the brothel!'

PALI'S WIVES

At the point that I married Pali, the American press resurrected my Ryan adventures once more. They discovered that Pali had been married and divorced three times.

They also wrote of him: 'Not only has Count Pálffy had three wives, but his secular life has been anything but a tranquil one. His marriages have been international sensations. He reached the climax in his second marriage – to the famous Dolly [Dorothy] Deacon whose mother's lover was killed by her father.' That was true! It happened in Cannes.

Pali's first wife, whom he married in 1915, was my mother's cousin. She was an Esterházy called Franziska-Romana, the daughter of my maternal grandmother's sister. She later married Prince Bela Odescalchi in Budapest.

His second wife was a Europeanised American, Princess Dorothy Radziwill, née Deacon, the youngest sister of Gladys, Duchess of Marlborough. They came from Boston, but had been brought up mainly in France. Some say that Dorothy was quite a minx and she seemed to have many bad qualities inherited from her mother, without that special brilliance that made Gladys so fascinating to the artists and intellectuals of her day. Pali used to tell me that Dorothy was terribly jealous.

Dorothy's early life was not designed to make her later life easy. She was born in 1891 when her parents' life was in rather a muddle. Her mother was having an affair with a Frenchman called Emile Abeille. Her father grew suspicious. The following spring he pursued his wife and Abeille to the Hotel Splendide in Cannes, and found Abeille cowering behind the sofa in Mrs Deacon's room. He fired three bullets at Abeille, who died in a pool of blood. Most unfortunate – and who knows whether that was his plan or whether things got out of hand?

The scandal that followed did not drive the family into the seclusion that habitually follows such incidents. Dorothy married Prince 'Aba' Radziwill in 1910, the marriage fiercely opposed by Aba's fat mother, known as 'Bichette'. None of the family attended the wedding. When Aba's father died in an insane asylum in Vienna in 1914, Dorothy discovered that 'Bichette' had paid Aba's extensive debts in exchange for the family estates at Nieswiesz, a few hundred miles south of St Petersburg. So Dorothy could not have what was rightfully hers.

Dorothy's marriage to Aba was overshadowed by 'Bichette', but eventually she was accepted by the family. By 1912 Mary Berenson was describing her as 'divinely beautiful but already false and spoilt.' Mrs Berenson also noted that she was 'a swan among ducks, for they are barbaric Poles thinly veneered with cosmopolitan *usages*.' A girl was born in 1917, called Betka. But a mere two years later, Dorothy ran away with Pali. The Radziwill divorce was difficult. It was finally annulled in Rome in 1921. She then married Pali in 1922. Very soon afterwards they had a son, Johnnie.

I recently found some letters that Dorothy wrote about their marriage, which might have given me cause for alarm had I read them before my own marriage. Some of these describe the great shoots they had, a life very similar to my own when I married Pali. Dorothy had twenty guests for four days at Christmas 1924 and they bagged 2,750 hares, 860 in one day with eight guns. But by the following June, Dorothy's marriage was in crisis, as she wrote to her uncle:

'I can put off no longer to tell you what is breaking my heart. My husband has left me. The whole thing is so horrible! The way it was done so disgusting, all this for a Greek girl of 22, a Mlle Mercati* whom I presented him to in Cannes. 3 days later she was living with him & the whole thing lasted 10 days! We came back here with the children & on last 15th, a week ago, he walked off to Paris to meet her. So now all is finished between him & I.

It is hard, I assure you to have one's life completely finished at 34, & to be alone with 2 small children. Pudmerice for the first time is looking so lovely. My destiny in life seems to be to plant gardens which I never see flower!... I shall never give him a divorce. Why should I break my children's home?

Of course I think he is crazy, for the day before he met *this* girl he was telling me how much in love he was with someone else! Perhaps this madness makes things all the more painful as it destroys so many illusions.'

By July Dorothy was more settled, resigned to doing nothing on account of her children and for what she called 'the great love I have had for Pali':

---

* Daria Mercati. She married four times and died tragically, burning to death in her bed in a Geneva hotel. Her sister, Atalanta, married the author, Michael Arlen, best remembered for his novel, *The Green Hat*.

First adventure. Etti as a lovelorn bride in New York 1933.

Left Etti's father, Count Ferdinand Wurmbrand – or was he her father?

Above Etti as a youngster.

Below left Etti's mother, the former May Baltazzi.

Below Maria Vetsera, Etti's cousin, murdered at Mayerling in 1889.

Aristides Baltazzi, gentleman rider, Derby winner, and Etti's grandfather.

Napajedla – the family stud in former Czechoslovakia.

Etti with her first great love – Count Vladschi Mittrovsky.

RYAN COUNTESS' LOVE SECRET BARED

Rich Marriage Rumors Used by Mother to Pacify Creditors

She was born into the Austrian nobility and before she was 20, her extravagant mother had her twice engaged to wealthy noblemen after courtships of two and three days.

Both bethrothals ended with the payment of large indemnities to the mother.

Expensive lingerie was ordered in exclusive European shops and even while it was being made one coat of arms was ordered ripped from it and another sewn on.

Why?

The Evening Journal begins today to tell from court and police records how the young and lovely Countess Clarisse Marietta Wurmbrand-Stuppach went from engagement to engagement, while her mother pacified creditors with the promise: "When my daughter marries I will pay you."

The daughter did not marry until Clendenin J. Ryan, Jr., grandson of Thomas Fortune Ryan, made her his bride in St. Patrick's Cathedral last February after knowing her only six weeks. He now is suing to annul the marriage.

On Sept. 11, 1933, the Countess Marie von Wurmbrand-Stuppach was arrested in a Vienna hotel by police of that city and taken to prison.

No American newspaper correspondent cabled the news of her arrest to his paper. Why should he? Who, then, was interested in the fact that a member of the Austrian nobility, the most ancient nobility in Europe, had been arrested charged with a commercial crime — the defrauding of creditors? No one—then.

Less than a year has passed, but now that same Countess, though he has never seen her, is the mother-in-law of Clendenin J. Ryan, Jr., grandson of Thomas Fortune Ryan and heir to some $8,000,000 of the latter's $115,000,000 estate. Her daughter, the lovely Clarisse Marietta von

RYAN COUNTESS LOVE COSTLY TO BARON

Continued from First Page.

Wurmbrand-Stuppach, married young Mr. Ryan in St. Patrick's Cathedral last February.

Wooed by Heir For Six Weeks

He had known her six weeks, a short courtship, perhaps. But a long one, a very long one, compared to the previous courtships which had resulted in her engagement to at least two men, her reported engagement to a third and the admiration felt for her by still a fourth.

Sinister headlines on the Ryan marriage. Inset at the top is 'Heir to a fortune' and husband no 1 – Clendenin Ryan, Jr.

Etti emerging from her American misadventure.

Etti in Hungary.

The Pálffy team of horses.

Pudemerice – one of the Pálffy castles
in Hungary.

Above left Etti with Pali Pálffy – husband no. 2. He created more Countesses than the Pope.

Above Etti with a large black buck, shot by her.

Left Etti on safari in India in 1936.

Below Etti with the Maharajah of Bikaner.

Above Cecilia Sternberg, shrewd observer of Etti's marital career.

Above right The favourite. Tommy Esterházy, husband no 3, with their daughter Bunny.

Right Etti in a carriage at Devescer with Yén, her faithful servant.

Below An interior of Devescer, one of the Esterházy residences.

'He, on his side is also giving up the idea, but not that nasty little ½ Greek ½ Jewess girl. His father has taken up the matter very seriously, has made his will leaving John in case this ½ of the property & in case of Pali's wanting to remarry the other ½ goes over to the boy also, Pali getting only *le légitime*. It would be both mean & untrue if I said that he was staying on with me only *pour raisons pecuniaires*, but naturally *celà est également mis dans la balance*....

My heart is *broken*, my hopes are shattered, my illusions completely destroyed & that of course shall never be able to be done over. Why is life so horrible & men such brutes?!'

By November that year (1925), the marriage had reached some brief stability, Dorothy writing:

'As for my situation towards Pali it has now at last taken the right direction. I believe he still writes to that impossible Greek girl, who by the way has left for America with her mother, Baroness Phlugel. I came back here on the 28th & to my astonishment I found Pali at the station awaiting me in Presbourg. Since then he is overwhelming me with affectionate demonstrations, but my heart has been so terribly hurt that I feel that it can never be the same again.'

Pali himself took a more optimistic view, writing to Dorothy's uncle in December:

'It's already weeks that I wanted to write you. But though I could have written you about the start & try of our new life, it's only today after over two months, that I can write about facts & results. I don't know if Dorothy has written you in general only or in details, but I make a point in telling you myself, that we lead a happier life now than any time before.

Having seen the near smash of our existences so near, we have both changed, have put our good wills together, putting aside '*les choses passées*', & found it much simpler than imagined to find each other again. We live a quiet happiness, without fights nor disagreeable words, finding pleasure in our sweet children & our home, which becomes nicer every day. These news, I am sure, will be the nicest X-mas message we can send you, as they will give you pleasure.'

Pali mentioned in his letter that he was too busy and too poor to go anywhere for a while, adding, without emphasising the point: 'Dorothy doesn't want to leave me all alone in Pudmerice again, realising how sad it is here in winter.'

For some time the marriage returned to normal, the Tzigane band playing and sport was the order of the day. They killed a thousand head of stag over the Christmas period. They fed 71 people (including servants). Before that Pali took Dorothy to the Károlyis at Totmegger, which he described as the best shoot in the world. There, in six days, with eight guns, they killed 10,000 heads, himself 1,200.

Dorothy's younger daughter, Caja, was born in Paris in 1927, but within a year all the good hopes that Pali and Dorothy had for their marriage came to nothing. She may have disposed of Daria Mercati, but soon there were sterner threats. In June 1928 Pali and Dorothy were divorced. Dorothy's legacy to Pali was malevolent. She persuaded his uncle to disinherit him. He left everything to his doctor, in whose family that part of the estate remains to this day.

Dorothy never remarried, but in August that year Pali married his third wife in Tyrnan. She was called Eleanor Greene Roelker. She was the daughter of William Roelker of Greene Farm, East Greenwich, Rhode Island, where her family had lived since 1680. In 1914 she had married Harrison Tweed, the senior partner of the New York law firm, Milbank, Tweed, Hope and Hadley. He later served as acting President of Sarah Lawrence College. They had two daughters*, and were divorced in 1928.

Eleanor was good looking in an American way, a long time

* One daughter, Eleanor became Mrs Nelson Aldrich; the younger, Katharine Winthrop, was the first wife of Archibald Roosevelt, Jr. (his 2nd being Selwa Showker – 'Lucky' Roosevelt). Tweed went on to marry Blanche Oelrichs Barrymore, the strange lesbian, known as 'Michael Strange'; after their divorce in 1942, he married Barbara Banning.

member of the Colony Club in New York, one of those smart Americans who find their way to Europe and are then so taken by its ways that they decide to try their luck with a European aristocrat as a husband. This could be blamed on the American columnist, Walter Lippmann, who was determined that she should study in Paris and make more of her life. There she met Pali. I myself met her several times and she was a charming person.

In later life Eleanor Tweed wrote stories for the *New Yorker* and other magazines. She wrote two books, both of them novels, but more by way of 'faction' – novels that are loosely based on fact. One of her books was about Isabella Stewart Gardner and John Singer Sargent, the other about her own life. The later book was called *Largely Fiction*. It was meant to be an autobiography and ended up 'part fact but largely fiction'. It gave an undisguised portrait of Pali himself. He was enraged by this, saying that she sensationalised their marriage and made up lurid stories. He wanted to sue her but couldn't. In the end he decided that 'largely fiction' was the only part of the book that had any veracity and left this as his comment on the book.

I have read *Largely Fiction* again recently and I must agree it is hard to know where fiction ends and fact takes over; but I had no trouble in recognising that social old priest of the Proustian circle, Abbé Mugnier, as one of the characters in her book.

I fear there is more than a little truth in the portrait of Pali too. Eleanor Tweed was impressed by Pali as a good-looking aristocrat, but feared him as a 'Bluebeard' figure.

I can see why Pali disliked the book. She has a facility for the disobliging remark. In the book the heroine meets the Pali figure (Count Béla) while travelling with her cousin Abigail:

> 'Boston did not delay in discovering that, though the ancestry was impeccable and the charm notorious, they were offset by certain liabilities: Count Béla's debts were as extensive as his wide acres, his *bonnes fortunes* more celebrated than the antlers on his walls. Worse, a wife or two lurked in the background.[1]

If we are to believe the story, Eleanor Tweed headed into the unknown territory of Hungary, a 'Black Protestant' hoping to marry a 'Black Catholic', but fearing that there would be no wedding if the groom were disinherited by his father. She found herself in a huge castle, with a variety of family relations resident in various parts, eighteen indoor servants, and at least two hundred workers on the estate.

She made some good points about the Pálffy circle. Bereft of political influence, they and their friends lived for sport. It was said that when they did have a political role, the Opposition always awaited the hunting season before presenting difficult legislation. In Eleanor's time, she claimed that when not hunting, the family engaged in extensive litigation amongst themselves, a similar sport in many ways. Hers is a funny book with interesting points made:

> 'Most Hungarians did not exercise for exercise's sake. It would never have occurred to them to do calisthenics or to run around the Charles River Basin. But given a gun or a Tzigane band they could stalk all day or dance the czárdás, the most athletic of dances, all night. How they managed to remain in training was a mystery. They could drink great quantities of wine and himbeer-schnapps or slivovics without showing it, and eat dumplings smothered in paprika and plums blown into heavy batter without putting on an ounce. [Pali] certainly put his guests over the jumps, and anyone who could not walk all day through the shoulder-high corn in the relentless August sun after partridges or do thirty kilometres over slippery, half-frozen ploughed fields in the rain and snow of a Slovakian December after hare would not be asked a second time.'[2]

Later her story takes a sinister turn. After four years of marriage, she went to Vienna to consult a Jewish doctor about her nose. She had been hit by her husband. They had argued about money – 'It is always money, not women, as people think.' She had slapped his face and he had knocked her out. Now she worried that he would no longer love her with a broken nose. Into the thoughts of the doctor, Eleanor Tweed put a summing up of

Pali:

'She's right, he was thinking, her husband wouldn't care for a woman with a broken nose, or with any other disfigurement. [Pali] didn't care for any *one* woman very long anyway. Her time was running out. Yes, it was several years since her marriage had rocked Viennese, even European society. Bluebeard was his nickname. People were beginning not to be able to remember his wives, just as they had long since ceased counting his official fiancées and all the other women.'3

The story then descends to hinting that the Pálffys were inbred, thus making them dangerous, and Pali high-tempered. From being hit, she claimed that her right eye developed inexplicable blinking. The eye had to be removed 'like the eye of a fish.' From an argument about money, the story was that it was in a moment of unreasonable jealousy that he hit her, because she had dined with her former fiancé in Paris. This is how she tells it:

'Watching him through a haze of exhaustion, she saw his pupils grow slitted, like a cat's. Then, spitting out a short word, he reached for the revolver.

Her hand got to the cartridges one split second before his did. As long as she lived she would hear the clatter of them on the hardwood floor. Long before their din had fallen away the great revolver came down over her temple with a crash. For the first time in her complacent life she knew the meaning of fear, the value of flight. She took to her heels, and locked and bolted the doors of her room.'4

After that, in *Largely Fiction*, the marriage between Pali and Eleanor gradually dissolved. So it was in life. They stayed married until October 1934, when they divorced without having children. There is one further reference in the book to her seeing him with her glass eye in Salzburg:

'Peering about Mary Elizabeth dimly noticed a tall man, slouched at a table with a pretty, tired woman.' He greets her as if they were still the best of friends: 'What do you think of my latest countess? Pretty, isn't she?'

The latest countess was me!

Apparently, in later life, Eleanor Tweed wore an eye patch and claimed that it was a blow from Pali that made this necessary. I can well see why Pali distanced himself from her book. It was not published until 1948, and fortunately, in the meantime I remained in ignorance of all that had passed before between Pali and other women.

Eleanor Tweed died in America in October 1952.

LIFE WITH PALI

Soon after my divorce from Clendenin Ryan, Pali and I became engaged. All this appeared in the newspapers in August 1935. New York was a nightmare soon forgotten. I exchanged the slick world of skyscrapers, cocktails and motorcars for a world of solid old castles, great antlers, men with handsome moustaches, and horses and carriages. It was a world I knew well and where I was much more at home.

Before we married, I came to know Pali's home, Pudmerice. We spent Easter there in 1935, then in Bratislava and without publicity, on 19 November, I became Pali's fourth wife. Hardly was the ceremony over than we departed on honeymoon for England. Of course there was the problem that we were only married civilly not religiously which some of Pali's less exciting relations understandably did not like.

We arrived at Eastwell Park, in Kent. This was once the home of Queen Victoria's son, the Duke of Edinburgh, and Queen Marie of Romania was born there. Then we went shooting with Lord Belper at his 250-acre Derbyshire estate, Kingston Hall. His fortune came from the cotton trade, his firm being W.G. and J. Strutt, and he was the father of Lavinia Strutt, who later married the Duke of Norfolk. We went on to Welbeck Abbey in Nottingham to stay with the old Duke of Portland. That was a fascinating house with a great network of underground rooms and passages constructed by the eccentric bachelor 5th Duke, with even the ballroom built below the ground. Our Duke had been Master of the Horse and took a keen interest in the fate of the Spanish Riding School in Vienna and the Lipizzaner horses, so dear to the heart of the Pálffy family.

We then came back to Bibersburg and Pudmerice for Christmas. Pudmerice was Pali's castle in the countryside about thirty-five kilometres from Pressburg-Bratislava between Budapest and Vienna. The huge castle, with its numerous rooms, was built in 1889, set in a large English-style park of a hundred hectares. Adjoining this, the plains stretched as far as the Little Carpathians. The castle was not especially beautiful, but it was extremely comfortable, thanks to the attentions of Pali's two American wives, who had installed a great number of bathrooms, a rarity in Europe in those days, and who had made sure that the place was the best heated in Europe.

Every morning ten barefoot housemaids raked the drive, smoothing it to perfection each morning. Life was formal and feudal, but very civilised. My room had a huge Empire style bed in which I slept, and it was not unusual to awake and find servants passing through the room. The many guest rooms were decorated in the Biedermeyer style and every one had its own bathroom.

At Christmas there was always a huge tree reaching up through the two storeys of the castle and all the family, household staff and children and the estate workers gathered in the hall before Midnight Mass. We would then lead the procession on foot to the church through the snow, guided at first by the moonlight and later by the Christmas trees in the cottage windows. Sometimes the winters were bitterly cold.

This was a good marriage. Pali was kind and easy to get along with. It was an ideal life. In the summer we had Lipizzaners and wonderful horses to drive out every day. Frequently there would be a small procession of carriages with two white Lipizzaner horses parked outside the castle like taxis to take our guests to the Carpathians. In the winter we went out in horse-drawn sleighs, the coachmen dressed in black in the old Hungarian style with long black ribbons hanging from their hats. I often drove out four-in-hand, both in summer and winter.

In the evenings our guests dined by candlelight, and after dinner the Tziganes came to play. Wherever Pali went he was followed by his Tziganes, who played for him. They were a band, rather like gypsies, but not gypsies, and they played in restaurants where we dined. He had two troupes of them, one for himself and his guests and another for the servants. Pali played the cymbals and his Tzigane band played with him. They were graded according to merit. The least good played outside the front door, the next best in the hall, while the virtuosos were dressed in dinner jackets and played in the dining room. So the house was always filled with music. They were never allowed to sit down. One night we were entertaining Frank Hutton, Barbara Hutton's father, and Pali got so annoyed that he picked up one of the musicians and threw him out of the window. I was there. I saw it.

We often went to Budapest or Vienna, visiting friends in the Diplomatic Corps and our various relations. Sometimes we went to visit Tommy Esterházy, the man who had promised my mother to repay her before I went to America. In Vienna Pali owned a share of the Three Hussars, a nightclub, and here we entertained the many Maharajahs who visited from India. One time the Maharani of Cooch Behar came. She was Aisha Jaipur's mother and she was quite a lady. She adored going to bed with attractive men. I think she went to bed with all the Austrians she met. In our circle we called her the Maharani of *Couche Partout*!

One evening there was a ball at the Polo Club in Vienna, a wild party and everyone rushed around holding hands. The Maharani was wearing a wonderful emerald necklace and during the wild dancing it broke and all the emeralds scattered in the garden on the lawn. The next morning all the Austrian counts were on their hands and knees, scrabbling about for the emeralds. They weren't intending to give them back to her, but the Maharani was unconcerned. 'Don't worry, it's all insured,' she said.

It was with Pali that I embarked on an energetic sporting life.

He taught me to shoot, and we spent much time in the beauty of the Carpathians, disappearing on regular pilgrimages there for two or three weeks at a time, the expedition entirely devoted to shooting. There was no telephone, no mail, nothing. We were completely cut off from the rest of the world. We went there to shoot beautiful stags. We went up very high into the mountains and stayed in small huts, and went out to shoot at dawn, sleeping out of doors in the afternoon. It was a healthy life, wonderful.

Pali was a legendary shot, one of the best in Europe, as well he might have been given the amount of time he devoted to the sport. He understood the stag and loved nothing better than to hear its call at 4 am. This he could imitate. He once pointed out a stag about a kilometre away and urged me to listen quietly. From his shoulder he took down a huge conch, put it to his mouth and blew. He made the perfect imitation of a rutting stag. Though far away, the stag threw back its head to answer. The beast recognised the sound as that of another rutting stag. Thus Pali was able to lure his rival towards him, and the stag was rather surprised when eventually, with his great antlers raised on high, he came face to face with my husband. Pali saluted him and they went their separate ways.

We had many guests with us in the Carpathians, the Jaipurs often coming to stay, and our English friend, Lord Belper. He was very English in his manner and an excellent shot. He had shot stags in Scotland and he had shot stags in New Zealand. He loved it in the Carpathians, but he was already a certain age. We were in different huts and we only met once a week.

One time I was in a hut with Lord Belper, who was much older than me. He had muscle trouble in one of his legs. I remember the sight of the ghillies massaging him. But we were worried about him. We were so far from anywhere. One year he brought his nephew with him. During that stay, it was foggy and rainy and we all decided to stay indoors, but the nephew said: 'I think I'll just go along for a walk with the ghillie into the woods and see what's happening.'

When he came back he had shot the biggest stag. He was just sitting outside quietly and he shot it. Sensational. He had never been in the Carpathians before. His uncle, Lord Belper, was so angry that he could not speak to him. He never addressed a word to him the whole time he was there. All because his nephew had shot a fantastic stag, better than his.

Frank Hutton would come to shoot. He was always drunk. He drank a lot. Sometimes we went to stay with Count Potocki, who had about a hundred servants all in livery. Princess Marina and the Duke of Kent stayed there for the weekend and said: 'How funny that these flowers are yellow today. Yesterday they were blue.' Count Potocki could not bear to see his gardeners working, so they did all their work at night. The borders had been replanted during the hours of darkness.

Count Potocki used to take us riding in the woods. We rode along one bridle path and then seemed to cross over where we had ridden before. But there were no hoof-prints or tracks of any kind. Confused, we asked Count Potocki: 'Alfred I don't see any hoof marks. Surely we came this way a few minutes ago.' The Count explained: 'I can't bear to see the tracks. I have servants concealed in the woods and as soon as we have passed, they come out and brush them away.'

INDIA

Pali took me to India two years running on tiger shooting expeditions for two or three months at a time. In 1936 we sailed to Bombay in the *Conte Verde*, the Lloyd Triestino liner built four years before. It was a lovely ship, very comfortable. I was sad to hear it had been capsized by its crew at Shanghai at the time of Pearl Harbor.

In India we moved from one Maharajah to the next. Our world was filled with stags and elephants, Maharajahs and vast palaces. Mainly we shot tigers, then there were the different kinds of antelope. Tiger shoots were very exciting. The Maharajahs owned such huge territories, each the size of a country. And there were no poachers in those days. Only the Maharajahs and their guests shot the game.

We were rarely in danger, except perhaps once. Tigers did not often mix with each other. The old tigers had their own territory and so when we went into a place where it looked as though there might be a tiger, though the gamekeepers did not know if it was going to be an old tiger or not. Naturally, they preferred to shoot the old tigers rather than the young ones. We found what is called a *gulla*, far away from anywhere, where there was water, therefore a likely home for a tiger. They put out an antelope or goat as bait and during the night the tiger came. The beaters heard his roar. They knew the bait had been taken.

In the morning all the beaters got into position and we went out at about eleven o'clock or midday, some sitting on an elephant, while Pali and I sat quietly near some trees. In front of us was a little lawn and then some more trees. The head gamekeeper was with us and he looked at the footprints and said: 'I think this must be a very old tiger!' Suddenly I looked behind us and the tiger was about twenty yards away, on the other side completely and he was already preparing to jump. He was enormous, very old, very big – a good tiger. Luckily Pali was a fabulous shot. He turned round and – Bang! Bang! – in one second. That was probably the nearest we came to being attacked.

It was very exciting being in a camp. At night we heard the tiger coming or the buffalo crashing through the camp. You have to have a feeling of danger. It makes it much more interesting.

Early on our trip we stayed with the old Maharajah of Bikaner. Sir Ganga Singh had reigned over his state since 1887, taking over when he was just a boy of seven. It was the second largest state in Rajputana and he had a reputation as an all-India statesman, who had served as a soldier under the British flag in three continents. To this day he is ranked as one of the twelve Indians who helped shape the political future of his country. One of the incredible things he did was to create the Gang Canal which brought the waters of the Sutlej to the desert. He lined it with concrete to prevent seepage in the porous soil and as a result, the population of Bikaner doubled as canal colonies sprang up, able at last to get water.

The Maharajah had fought in the Boxer operations in China in 1901 and was forever helping the British in their various war efforts. He was farsighted and keen to help break down the isolation in which many of the Indian princes then lived. It was he who persuaded the Viceroy, Lord Hardinge, to set up the annual Viceroy's conference.

He loved wildlife but Bikaner itself had little big game. There were no tigers there at all, yet he was credited with having shot more than 150 of them in the neighbouring jungles of Kotah, Gwalior, Bhopal and Datia, and in Nepal. He was famed for the sand grouse and wild duck shoots that he organised at the country residence he had built himself at Gajner, twenty miles from the capital. Gajner was a beautiful place with its palace on the lake and deer parks, and there were often as many as a hundred guests.

The Maharajah loved to entertain friends from overseas, and it was considered a particular honour if he arranged a shoot for you. It was while we were his guests at Gajner, that I shot a record antelope. The Maharajah had one surviving son, Sir Sadul Singh, who earned a reputation as one of the greatest shots in India. He fell terribly in love with me. One day he took me aside and said: 'May I kiss you?' So sweet. We went out and saw all the gazelles all around and he said to his shikari: 'The Countess will shoot one of the gazelles.' So I shot one and it was a record. The old Maharajah was not terribly pleased about it since it was one of the best ever shot.

One shooting party of Maharajahs followed another. From Bikaner we went to Kotah, and then to Narsingarh. The bag invariably consisted of Black Buck, Chinkara, Houbara, and sand grouse.

We travelled on to Gwalior, where Pali shot a 9 foot 5 inch tiger. In Delhi we saw thousands of Mohamedans at prayer in long neat rows. We visited Agra and saw the Taj Mahal, and the Red Fort. This reminds me of the relentless socialite, Sibyl Colefax, who was asked whether she had enjoyed her visit to India. 'Ah,' she said. 'You have no idea how wonderful it was to see the Aga Khan by moonlight!'

We went to stay with our friend, the Maharani of Cooch Behar at Woodlands, her Victorian Gothic mansion near Calcutta. The Maharajah sent his special train to take us to Calcutta where we were met by his silver Rolls-Royce. That was a 100-acre estate with stables for thirty horses, a huge lawn and nursery, cricket ground, and two tennis courts. The garage could hold twenty cars. We saw a goat sacrifice and the bathing of the Hatis (elephants). There was a panther beat, for which we went out into the bush on elephants. We stood in baskets on the top of the elephants, and from this vantage point Pali shot a panther. In the jungle of Cooch Behar the elephants waded through the water, in search of tigers and rhinos.

We also visited Benares and saw the natives bathing in the Ganges, and the strange ceremony of the burning of the dead by the side of the river. After Kapurthala, we went to Patiala, where I shot a big panther and Pali shot a Chital. In Bhopal I shot three tigers in one beat. And finally we saw the Buddhist monuments at Sanshi.

Pali and I returned home to Hungary in the Lloyd Triestino ship, *Victoria I*, the best of their liners, where we were well treated as Pali's stepfather was president of the line. We brought many trophies home with us – the tigers and other animals to be mounted as spoils at Pudmerice.

Besides India, we also went each year to Africa, which instilled a love and appreciation of danger into me. I love nature. Of course you shouldn't go to Africa now. It is a shame, but if anything happens to you, and you go to the hospital you are sure to get AIDs. I wanted to go there recently with my daughter, but my doctor advised against it. So you miss so much – the hyenas, wonderful animals, very ugly – and both the male and female carrying their young for miles in their mouths. Sometimes you would see a lot, and sometimes nothing – depending on the moon.

BERLIN LIFE

Berlin was wonderful in those days. Obviously I do not suggest that the Nazis were to be admired, but at that time we did not know all the terrible things that were happening. I just mean that from the point of view of a certain way of life, everything was beautifully run. I met many of the leaders who later went down in history as villains. I thought Göring was charming, if fat, while Goebbels, I must say, was likeable and intelligent. Göring came from a good family and was related to all the good, bourgeois people and some of the aristocracy. I do not think he knew about the concentration camps.

Berlin was the centre of social life in Germany at this time. There were beautiful parties given by Freddy and Lali Horstmann at their house in the Tiergartenstrasse. Freddy Horstmann was a connoisseur of beautiful objects and a most discriminating if lavish collector, whose fortune derived from his family's ownership of the Frankfurt newspaper, *General Anzeiger*. He was powerfully built, with a round, intelligent face, a sea captain's beard, and bushy eyebrows. His wife Lali was rich too, being the daughter of the banker, Paul von Schwabach and his wife, a Schroeder. She had special beauty with her white forehead and raven locks, and eager, vivid eyes. She fell in love with Freddy when she was sixteen, twenty years his junior, and sometimes appeared so young that she could have been his daughter.

Their dinners were fabulous. They served hot *foie gras*, cooked with apples and rice, their veal so rare that it could have been the tenderest bird's flesh, and they often finished their dinners with a delicious soufflé. Sometimes, after dinner, Freddy would bid the footmen bring in his favourite pieces of Augsburg gold and silver plate and tureens, as if it were a scene in a ballet. Then he would summon other treasures to be borne into the room – his favourite porcelain horse, a unicorn or some fine Dresden swans, made originally for the Tsar. After the Great War, Freddy had bought many princely collections, including vermeil. He loved themes for his parties. He would mix water-lilies brought by car from the Buckow lake with similar ones made of Berlin porcelain, or put real humming-birds in a gilded cage with Dresden china parrots.

Freddy was a great host and a great jester. One of his protegées was an impoverished Mexican girl called Gloria Rubio, who became a friend of mine at this time. She was born in Guadalajara and was one of the great beauties of her time with her dark hair, enormous dark eyes, and special beauty in her unique gestures. Gloria had begun life as a hostess in a Mexican nightclub, but had married a first husband called Scholtens and found her way to Germany. As I later discovered, Gloria had a wonderful sense of humour, great charm and a kind heart.

One night Freddy dressed her up and presented her at a dinner as a mysterious aristocrat. Count Franz Egon von Fürstenberg-Herdringen fell in love with her and married her. He was heir to beautiful estates in Westphalia and in order to marry her had to renounce his family succession rights, because of Gloria's first marriage. They settled in Berlin where they entertained a great deal. Later the Nazis watched them closely because of the international social set around them. Some people said she was a spy for the Allies, but they said that about many international people. Maybe she was. It did not concern me. Gloria reappeared in my life after the war, by which time she was a renowned hostess in jet set society as Mrs Loel Guinness.

Von Ribbentrop used to attend Freddy's parties. He offered Freddy the position of Head of the Foreign Ministry Chancery, which would have been ideal for him, but to it was attached the condition that he divorce his half-Jewish wife. Freddy preferred to resign, sacrificing his diplomatic career, to which he was devoted.

Freddy adored his possessions and held his own life as nothing compared to them. During the war they retreated to their property at Kerzendorf, and later to the agent's house on the estate. Freddy would not leave his collection and refused to believe that he was in danger. At the end of the war, the Russians advanced and he was taken in for questioning. He died of starvation in a concentration camp. Those days at Kerzendorf and the loss of Freddy was a story movingly told by Lali in her book, *Nothing for Tears*, which was remarkable in being totally free from a hint of self-pity. After the war she went to England, and later visited São Paulo, Brazil, where she died of a sudden massive heart attack in August 1954.

But back to happier times so far as the Horstmanns were concerned. Pali and I went to a magnificent party hosted by Freddy. For this particular evening Freddy specified that all the ladies should wear white evening gowns. I had not brought one to Berlin, so Freddy sent one round at once, which I kept.

Of course all this entertaining and being entertained was expensive. Pali did not seem to care. I soon realised that we were spending too much. Pali was a generous host. He financed his life by selling off parts of his huge estate, one after the other. I never knew the boundaries, but one day at Pudmerice Pali stretched out his arm with an expansive gesture towards the far distance and announced: 'All this – and far beyond the horizon – is mine!' But a relative of his sitting near me whispered: 'That land was sold just last week.' Pali was grand, he was an optimist. That was what I liked about him. He spread joy and happiness wherever he went. Things were all right at the moment, but I wondered silently how much longer he would be able to afford this seemingly limitless generosity.

THE INTERNATIONAL GAME EXHIBITION – 1937

It was not easy being married to Pali. He was so good looking that every woman was after him. Our marriage, though a happy one, was not destined to last long. When we went to Berlin in

November 1937 I had no idea how near the end it was.

The International Game Exhibition was our reason for going to Berlin. This was a fabulous event staged by Hermann Göring, under the aegis of le Conseil Internationale de Chasse and the first major international gathering of sporting figures since Vienna in 1910. The exhibition included prints and photographs of a huge variety of sports from pig sticking to fox hunting and small game shooting. There were guns and fishing tackle on display and even a special exhibit on falconry, which was then the rage in Germany. Needless to say, amongst the ten thousand trophies, there were 1,400 mighty antlers of continental red deer, which competed well with the wapiti of America. The finest head on show was the antlers of a red deer, spanning 75½ inches and some 47½ inches in length, which lived normally in Moritzburg in Saxony and dated back to 1586. King George V sent two elephant tusks over from England and Lord Belper contributed a magnificent stag shot in New Zealand.

Besides what was on show, it was an opportunity for sportsmen from all over the world to gather and share their reminiscences. These men in their forest-green coats, their hats adorned with little 'shaving-brush' tufts, moved about inspecting the trophies like art experts at a private view. While Göring was President of the German Association, Pali was President of the Hungarian side.

We met Göring on the first day at a lunch at his presidential palace. He made a speech saying how honoured he was to have such a distinguished hunter as Pali as his guest. Pali replied in his Austrian-German, which many probably did not understand. I was shocked by the way Göring dressed. He could have been in a Wagnerian opera, with his long green suede jacket, patent leather riding boots on his fat legs, and then his silver belt with a buckle inlaid with precious stones, mostly diamonds but some emeralds – to match the green of his coat. From this hung a small dagger, similarly adorned with diamonds and emeralds. I thought how our Maharajah friends were often picturesquely dressed, the difference being that their clothes had good taste.

It was obvious that Göring and his henchmen were using the occasion of this gathering to advance the Nazi cause, but Pali was a Hungarian aristocrat and no German, let alone a Nazi, would impress him. Göring opened the exhibition and spoke of the need to preserve wild life and of the good comradeship of the field. He spoke of the great improvements in the manufacture of guns, and of the new Reich game laws. He said: 'Everywhere you will find a determined effort now being made both to preserve wildlife and perfect the various species.'

There were many entertainments, a gala performance of the opera, *Freischütz*, displays of hound trailing and retriever trials, while some of the guests moved on to Brunswick for further festivities. A falconer on horseback sent his hawk off to kill and then called it back to his fist with a whistle and it sat there, contentedly eating its prey while the spectators looked on. Wild boar and deer were hunted and small game was shot.

Göring invited us on a stag shoot in the forest near Berlin. I was the only woman, and there were twenty men, all of them official representatives from the different countries, England, France and so on. I went out to shoot my stag and I overheard the keepers saying: 'I wonder which stag she will shoot? Will it be Hanzi or Franzi?' All the stags were so well known to them that they had names! This was somewhat off-putting, but I shot my stag. Frank Wallace, of the Shikar Club, who was there, failed to kill his stag. He wounded it. He was the only one to commit that crime.

Göring opened the Berlin Schloss for a great dinner, and adorned it with great paintings borrowed from museums. It was a glorious evening, and I sat next to him and to Prince Mecklenburg. As a woman I felt I could tease Göring about his clothes and his jewels. This he took quite well as I doubt many women teased him. I am afraid that I thought him no better than a clown, though I detected a hard and wicked look in his eyes, which made me realise that there was more to him. He was dangerous. Perhaps naively I raised the question of the Jews with him, telling him we had many Jewish friends. He did not reply and after the speeches he turned to the lady on his other side. Then there was a series of fanfares, after which no further conversation was possible.

This dinner was a disaster for some of the guests, including me. Lobster was served, which came from Horcher, the famous Berlin restaurant, where, incidentally, the restaurateur, Otto Horcher was a well-known spy for the Nazis with microphones concealed under the tables. These lobsters had been kept for a few days and had been re-heated. Out they came on gold plates. Lobster must be eaten right away, so some of the lobsters were poisonous and many of the guests fell ill after it. I was terribly sick for some days at the Hotel Adlon, lying in bed feeling ill while being bothered by questions from the German police.

LOUISE DE VILMORIN

I still had no idea that my marriage was in trouble. Just before the opening of the International Game Exhibition, Pali had visited Paris. He went there on his own and his friends, Élie de Talleyrand and Élie de Gaigneron gave a dinner for him at the Crillon.

Drifting about Paris at this time was a temptress determined to do me harm. Louise de Vilmorin was a legendary *femme fatale*. For some years this woman had been lurking in the background as a threat to our marriage. She was not horrible, she was cultivated and attractive, but she was horrible in the way that she played around with human beings. When she liked a man she would announce that she was going to bed with him. She destroyed marriages and not only mine. Probably the best known of her later conquests was Duff Cooper when he was Ambassador in Paris. She fell ill at the British Embassy, took to her bed and remained a guest of the Coopers for several years. Diana Cooper admired her as much as Duff. In later life Louise boasted of her triumphs. 'I had Duff, I had Diana, but never together,' she announced lazily.

For some reason Louise hated me. She went so far as to tell me so: 'I hate you and I am going to destroy your life.'

Louise was twelve years older than me and walked with a limp, which somehow made her the more alluring. She was to become one of France's most praised literary figures. Her family ran a seed-growing company, which was nothing to write home about, and her mother had been involved with King Alfonso XIII of Spain. My grandmother told me that she liked to sleep in black sheets. I thought this rather amusing, but my nurse said this was just to cut down on washing expenses, which did not entirely convince me. I always preferred white or pink sheets, especially pink ones and my maid used to make my bed with these wherever we went – in hotels and even in the sleeping cars of trains.

As a young woman she fell into a group of writers such as Antoine de St. Exupéry, Jean Cocteau and André Malraux. It was Malraux who encouraged her to write and as early as 1934 she published her first book, *Sainte Unefois*. This was one of about twenty books, which had considerable success in France and even in England. But I do not talk of her creations, rather of her destructions.

It is hard for me to define her charm, but others were captivated by the things she said. There were those who spoke of her warm-hearted friendship, her vivacity, her wit and her zest for life. John Julius Norwich called each of her books 'a little masterpiece'. He saw a poetic quality in her talk, describing her French as 'soft, beautifully articulated, with a strange sinuous quality about it . . .' He wrote: 'When she talked her words acted like a magic incantation. Spellbound, one listened: and soon, helplessly, one began to laugh.' Lord Norwich had another story about her, of an admirer who asked how old she was. '*Cher Monsieur*,' she replied, tapping the side of her forefinger against her cheek, '*ça dépend du jour.*'

I prefer Evelyn Waugh's version of her: 'a Hungarian Countess who pretended to be a French poet. An egocentric maniac with the eyes of a witch.' Nancy Mitford thought her 'vicious' and told Evelyn Waugh that she had shocked a friend of hers at a dinner party when the girls went upstairs to brush their hair. She said to them: 'This is just what I like, two pretty women. Get into bed girls and we'll have a *ménage à trois*.' The friend wanted to leave the house at once.

As I say, I never fully understood Louise's charm. Part of it was her originality. But when she wanted to seduce a man, she invariably succeeded. Whatever one might think of her and her ability to charm, she was certainly not the kind of woman that a wife would wish her husband to meet on a lone trip to Paris. But this is what happened to Pali. As I have made clear, Pali was a great huntsman, amongst the greatest of the century. His philosophy in regard to animals and also to humans was remarkably similar. He went in pursuit. If the beast moved on four legs he shot it. If on two legs, then he possessed her. Unfortunately for me, on this visit to Paris, it was Pali who found himself hunted.

Louise de Vilmorin was instantly taken with him – a *coup de foudre*. Pali, as again we have seen, was a man whose head was easily turned. Two days later Louise took a plane to Vienna to be with him. Pali went to her room at the Bristol to take her out to dinner. After dinner the Tziganes played for her. He stayed with her until seven the next morning and was with her again the following day.

While I was ill with food poisoning after Göring's dinner, Pali went to dinner at the French Embassy. I would have loved to have gone as I longed to inaugurate a brand new Coco Chanel dress. But I did not want him moping by my bedside so I told him to go. Louise was there. Presently Louise and Pali were to be seen dining at Horcher's, dancing at Ciro's, and it seems he was struck by her '*esprit français*', of which as a child of nature in Hungary he possessed none. I did not mind this, as I liked him to be happy and to have fun.

One day he came to my bedside, a place he had somewhat

deserted, turned his bright blue eyes on me and said: 'Etti, I'm in love with Louise.' As he never did things by halves, I knew at once that this meant he wanted to marry her. Even then he acted generously. He told my mother that she and I could continue to live at Pudmerice if we wished – even after the divorce and remarriage. We did not.

Pali and I were divorced in December and immediately after that he married Louise, his fifth wife. Years later he felt the need to explain why he rushed into another marriage, so soon after surrendering a previous wife. He thought he had found the woman of his life, to whom he would be married forever. It was always like that in his head, but in reality it seldom lasted longer than three years, and then there was another one. I was already his fourth wife, and others would follow. He also claimed that he had an urgent need to be married since his mother had divorced his father while he was a child. He craved family life, he said. He refused to accept that a man who married so often could be described as irresponsible or superficial. Rather, he was ruled by a sense of optimism or an unfortunate sense of idealism.

Of this turn of fate, I could but be philosophical. You couldn't hate Louise. I did not like her. She played with people's lives in her love of the game of seduction. It is even said that she seduced her brother, André.

PALI'S LATER WIVES

I might just mention that following Louise, Pali's unquenched desire for family life led him into three more marriages. There was one called Edith Hoch. I don't know what happened to her, but they got divorced. In 1951 he married Marie-Theresa, Grafin zu Herberstein-Proskaw. They were divorced in 1956. His last wife, whom he married that same year, was Carin Braun von Stumm. She gave him a second son called Andor, born in 1957.

Pali was such an attractive man that it was impossible to hold a grudge against him any more than Louise. His character was larger than life. I remember that when another of the family was having a disagreement with Pali's son Johnnie, he described this rather well. 'Johnnie was Pali's son,' he said. 'But the wine in the bottle is not the same!' When I was married to Arpad, we often saw Pali. He died in Munich in 1968.

Having lost Pali to Louise, I had no reason to suppose that she would play any further part in my life. In this not unreasonable hope I was to be hideously deceived.

SIX

Husband 3
Count Thomas Esterházy, 1938-1944

Count Thomas Esterházy von Galántha (1901-64)
Born Tata, Austro-Hungarian Empire, 25 December 1901.
Married Budapest, 5 March 1938, Countess Etti Wurmbrand.
Divorced 1944. One daughter.
Died Schruns, Austria, 6 December 1964.

THE LOSS OF Pali to Louise was a bruising experience. I was very unhappy for a while. I did not want to be single, and I was not single for long. Fortunately Thomas Esterházy, another Hungarian Count, came into my life. He had been in love with me for some time.

Tommy arrived in Berlin and Pali told him I was ill. He came to see me often. When I recovered, he took me out every day to Horcher's and we danced at Ciro's. When we discovered that Pali and Louise were going to those places, we went to Peltzer's and danced at the Quartier Latin. He sent me lovely flowers and when it was clear that Pali had settled for Louise with no further doubts, and wanted a divorce, Tommy asked me to marry him.

I was swiftly divorced from Pali in December 1937 and equally quickly remarried. On 5 March 1938 I married Tommy Esterházy, the nephew of my grandmother's sister and a member of the most distinguished family in Central Europe. His mother was a Lobkowitz from Bohemia, a distant relation of ours, and he had the typical Lobkowitz eyes. He was more a Lobkowitz than an Esterházy, which I rather liked – especially as I had had my fill of brave Magyárs.

I adored Tommy and consider him to be the most interesting of my six husbands. He was a lovely person in every way – easy-going, charming, very good looking and cultured. He was the opposite to Pali – loving beautiful things, and he was always elegantly dressed, with an original mind. He was old fashioned and had a valet who washed him and dressed him. He lived in wonderful style. He was so well looked after that he would just put out his foot, and one of the servants would put his shoe on for him, and tie the laces. But the best part of his character was that he was a kind person, very considerate and thoughtful.

Tommy had two castles, both estates adjoining and consisting together of 80,000 hectares. Pápa was a large 18th century house, which reminded me of Napajedla. He hardly ever lived there as even in those days it needed too many servants to run it, and he much preferred Devescer, the estate near the Balaton Lake, where we had so often visited for shooting parties. Devescer was the comfortable home. It was an old *Wasserburg*, and one of the most enchanting castles in Hungary.

Pápa was run as a kind of museum. We took our guests over to show them the treasures. It was full of beautiful furniture which the Esterházys had bought at the sales at Versailles soon after the French Revolution in 1789. They were the largest buyers at those sales, but the English Royal Family also bought a lot. They had chosen what to buy but nobody at the English court could speak good enough French to feel confident at bidding. Eventually they sent their French chef to represent them!

While the name of Pálffy is an ancient one, it does not bear the fame of that of Esterházy. This aristocratic Magyár family produced many generations of Hungarian diplomats, politicians and patrons of the arts. The family dates back to the early 13th century. They became princes of the German Empire in the 17th century and were staunch supporters of the Hapsburgs.

The first member of the family to achieve political importance was Ferenc Zerházy and he it was who changed the name to

Esterházy. Amongst their most famous antecedents were Paul Esterházy IV (1635-1713), a poet, harpsichordist, and composer, Prince Paul Anton (1711-62), who became a Field Marshal and first engaged Haydn. His brother, Nikolaus Joseph (1714-1790), was a general and diplomatist as well as patron of art, music and literature. He inherited Haydn from his brother, commissioned him to write chamber music for the baryton, and was behind a number of symphonies, though less interested in his string quartets.

Then there was Nikolaus Esterházy IV (1765-1833), the founder of the famous collection of pictures in Vienna and the man who declined Napoleon's offer of the Crown of Hungary. He commissioned the six late masses of Haydn, and Beethoven's Mass in C, but I am afraid he ventured to criticise the mass at its first performance, and Beethoven stormed out.

My marriage with Tommy lasted seven years and was full and interesting. Life was really marvellous, with a lot of shooting, travelling and huge house parties. We had a charming guest house near the castle where guests could be completely independent if they wished. They could play tennis, go riding or swimming, or be with us. There were wonderful forests for hunting and we invariably rose early for sport.

We had an excellent chef called Yén. Tommy was quite an artist with food and discussed each dish with him in long conversations in the morning. There were hundreds of servants. We were well looked after. It is only about ten years ago that I realised that servants had days off! In the evenings the servants were lined up all the way from the drawing room to our bedrooms in two rows, even late at night. It was picturesque and traditional, but I abolished this tradition as it was too exaggerated. I believe the tradition continued at Kesthely, the home of Prince Georgie Festetics but I never saw it myself as Tommy and I were not invited there, not having been married in church.

We had many visitors, in particular diplomats from Budapest and Vienna, as well as visitors from England, France, Germany and Italy. Towards the late 1930s when the political situation deteriorated and war approached, Devescer was a haven where diplomats could talk to each other safely and in the privacy of a weekend party. We particularly liked John F. Montgomery, the American Ambassador to Hungary, who was later such a help to Hungarians. And my sister, Sophia, had married Reinhard Henschel in November 1940. He was with the German Legation. He was from the family that built locomotives, aeroplanes and lorries.

The Italians afforded us great entertainment, but they never remained long *en poste*, due to their habit of having love affairs with Hungarian ladies. The Marchese Talamo fell for the wife of one of the four Keepers of the Crown of St Stephen. Though she was very beautiful, this was going too far. The thousand-year old Crown was venerated as a relic, and in the absence of a King since the end of the First World War, it was kept by four aristocrats who wore beautiful uniforms. The Marchese's wife left Hungary, and it was not long before he was recalled.

Another legendary figure was Mario Panza, an Italian diplomat, who was known as a most successful seducer of women. He arrived in Budapest at the outset of the war, still leading a life of considerable style, bringing with him about six polo ponies from his last posting in Brussels. He had an American wife, Janie, and when they came to stay, they arrived in two cars, one for them, the second for the luggage, the valet and the maid.

One English visitor was Unity Mitford, one of the famous Mitford sisters, the one who loved Hitler. We were not sure whether or not she was sleeping with Hitler. The fact that there was gossip about this amongst her friends gave her a certain *cachet*. She was then the close friend of Count Janos Almasy, and came to stay with us in 1939. Her story is well known. She shot herself in the temple in the English garden in Munich and was taken home, a pathetic invalid, maimed for her obsession with the Nazi regime. She died while in the care of her family in 1948.

Admiral Nicholas Horthy, Regent of Hungary, was another

visitor. After some years in the back seat of politics, he had taken control since 1937 and was initially sympathetic to Hitler's crusade against Bolshevism, while disliking Hitler himself. During the war he began by keeping Hungary aloof from involvement, but in 1941 he led Hungarian forces against Yugoslavia and in November that year signed the German-Italian-Japanese pact, thus siding with the Axis powers. Hitler tried to trick him into declaring war against the British and American allies, but he refused. (Later on, in 1944, Hitler invaded Hungary and Horthy asked for an armistice and retired from public life).

Before all that, in easier times, Horthy came to shoot, as did Prince Albrecht of Bavaria. There was an occasion when they were both present at the same party. Prince Albrecht, who loved animals, found a little roe deer and gave it to me to put in one of the guest rooms of the lodges we used for our visitors. The room chosen by Horthy was the easiest place to put it. I gave it some milk and completely forgot about it. Horthy arrived, surrounded by his staff, and on opening the door to his room, was amused to see the little deer lying on his bed.

We had one daughter, Marianne Berta Felicie Johanna Ghislaine Theodora Huberta Georgina Helene Genoveva, always known as 'Bunny'. She was born in Budapest on 12 December 1938. Of course I did not look after Bunny myself when she was little. We had lovely English nurses. One of them had been nurse to the Queen and Princess Margaret and she loved dogs. So there were always dogs in the nursery. We were not very happy about that, but she assured us that in England babies and dogs were always together. It was so funny.

I know that I was neither a good nor attentive mother. Both Tommy and I adored Bunny, but we either left her with the nannies or despatched her to stay with friends. I did not travel with Bunny at this time because I was short of money.

IN LOVE AND WAR

In 1941 my new life stretched before me with infinite possibilities of lasting happiness. The outbreak of the Second World War in September 1939 at first had little impact on our lives. The shooting parties and house parties continued as before, and we made a point of continuing to entertain the various diplomats, with the background thought that perhaps if we were in trouble they would help us. To be honest, we did not think we would need help. We were blind to the dangers encroaching on our lives. Most of us were in sympathy with the Allies and we had a dream that one day the British Army would march in from the South, perhaps with old Churchill riding at its head, and release Hungary from the dangers of the Nazis and the Russians. Only my mother, ever a canny Greek, thought otherwise. She warned us continually what was likely to happen. My brother-in-law, Reinhard Henschel, was recalled to the Foreign Ministry in Berlin, and they left their little son, Federick, to be brought up at Devescer with Bunny. Despite the war, our English nurse stayed on to look after the children and taught them to sing 'God Save the King' and 'Rule Britannia'.

The only inconvenience in our lives was a social one, the proximity of Pali Pálffy and his new wife Louise. We all moved in the same aristocratic circles, but there developed an unwritten rule that the hostesses in Budapest never asked the Pálffys and ourselves to the same dinners. They could hardly expect me to go to a party where Louise de Vilmorin was to be with my former husband. This I would not have minded though there were a few residual problems over money between me and Pali. My former husband made a point of keeping on good terms with his ex-wives, fiancées, mistresses and flirts, a wise philosophy on his part since he amassed so many of them. Louise de Vilmorin would no doubt have enjoyed the irony of the four of us being together in one room, though even she kept her distance. She sensed that Tommy was intensely hostile to her, out of his loyalty to me. So we did not meet.

Early in 1942 I departed for Rome, while Tommy told me he had to stay in Budapest for business reasons and would join me later. He did not do so, and I became a bit concerned as I was aware that he was not a gifted businessman. He used to offer to buy me jewels but I declined, urging him to invest the money in his estates. Like Pali he was spending too much, and the estates badly needed fresh capital. I persuaded him to buy a beautiful fruit-growing estate near Devescer and put it in Bunny's name so that she would have something later on.

While in Rome I wondered what he was doing in Budapest. When, after two months, I returned, I found the city awash with rumours. 'Tommy has been flirting with Louise de Vilmorin!' my friends told me. Presently the story became clear.

Louise was apparently happily married to Pali, but she was a cosmopolitan creature, who yearned for the literary life of Paris. Her books were beginning to be published with some success. Pali's mother was killed in a car accident not long after she settled at Pudmerice and whereas previously the house was filled with guests, it was veiled in mourning for six long months. The telephone never rang, there were no guests. Louise began to kick her heels in boredom. During these years Pali had several 'flirts' which did not concern Louise unduly. She knew the nature of the beast. But anyone who knew Louise would have sensed that her capricious nature would soon lead her into further adventures and mischief.

Louise happened to be alone in Budapest in February 1942, while Pali was occupied on his estates. Princess Marie (Marizza), born Andrassy, the wife of Prince Johannes of Liechtenstein, a distant cousin of the reigning Prince, invited her to dinner. Louise had already promised to dine with the Dampierres (Robert being counsellor at the French Embassy), but she agreed to join Marizza at midnight.

When Louise arrived, she found Marizza alone with Tommy and after ten minutes or so, the three of them left for the Colonial

Bar. It did not take Louise long to discover that I was safely out of the way in Rome. She had developed a penchant for Hungarian counts. Already bored with her life and restless for mischief, this knowledge freed her to set about seducing my husband. Louise and Tommy talked until three in the morning, during which I am assured he did not flirt with her, merely talked of many aspects of life. Finally he deposited her at the door of her house where he told her: 'I can't understand you. For me you are more than a devil. Nothing real matters to you.' She excused herself and went inside.

Tommy must have fallen under her spell. A little later, well after 3 am we must remember, he telephoned Louise and said: 'I am ringing you because I am sure that if I did not telephone, you would not call me and we would never see each other again after an evening where we have at last met.' They talked until 4.30 when Tommy heard her yawn. She told him she was hungry and he offered to bring her some *foie gras*, bread and butter. A few minutes later he was at her house and thus began their love affair.

Apparently Louise thought she could seduce Tommy by masquerading as a Hungarian. She bought a Hungarian fur coat, called a Roznoy coat, and a blanket with wolves' fur for her bed. But Tommy was not drawn to Magyár tastes, he did not even care for gipsy music. He was more of an Austrian. He was not going to be drawn by Louise singing Hungarian songs. So she changed her tactics and behaved like an Austrian lady, which again, of course, she was not.

I was still in Rome but Pali heard about Tommy's infatuation and evidently thought it amusing. He did not feel threatened by the situation and it never crossed his mind that the pair might be lovers. He even thought that when I returned to Budapest, I would be delighted to find them all such good friends.

In March Louise left for Paris to launch her book, *Lit á Colonnes*. She was away until 22 April during which time she and Tommy often wrote to each other. Meanwhile I returned to hear all the rumours and was forced to confront Tommy and ask him what was going on. To my horror he confessed that he was completely stricken with the forty-year-old Louise. I was devastated but hoped that perhaps Tommy might tire of Louise and return to me. I did not even mind that he had given her some family jewels, which should have been reserved for the primogeniture.

It was not long before I discovered a cache of love letters locked in Tommy's desk and in my despair, I went with them to Pali to ask him how we should deal with the situation.

When Louise returned to Pudmerice, Pali confronted her with these letters and far from being ashamed of her affair, she stood her ground and accused him of breaking their marriage by producing them. Her code was that it was acceptable to have an affair, but not acceptable to confront someone with the evidence. In other words, affairs were not what broke marriages, but presenting documentary proof was.

Pali asked me to be with him when Louise came home from Budapest (and her affair with Tommy). Thus I joined him at Glamb Utca and we awaited her return. A bitter argument ensued which resulted in the collapse of both marriages. While Louise was apparently happy to continue seeing Tommy secretly, he wanted to divorce me and marry her. Pali resolved any future problems of loneliness by embarking on a new love affair with a pretty brunette girl with whom he was frequently spotted in the restaurants. I was deserted and, soon afterwards, divorce proceedings began.

Years later, Louise used to boast with pride that she had stolen two husbands from me. I still could not hate her, since it is not in my nature to hate anyone. But I was shocked by the insouciant way in which she played with the lives of others.

Louise left Pali and eloped with Tommy, but this time she did not marry my husband. Theirs was not an easy fate. It was wartime. The political situation deteriorated in Germany, particularly after the Germans' defeat at El Alamein. Both Louise and Tommy got stuck in Hungary, though they often visited

Berlin and were entertained by the Horstmanns as if they were man and wife.

By February 1943 Louise had come to the conclusion that life in Hungary was too dangerous, and that if she did not leave then, she might never get out. She may well have been right. She returned to Paris, eventually settling at Verrières, her home near there, while Tommy stayed on in Hungary. Apart from a brief time in Budapest at the beginning of 1944, they were separated for the next two years. Tommy did not return to me at Devescer. His pride was hurt and he went on living in Budapest.

Life was very different. The diplomats had largely been recalled or left, and I never went to the German Legation any more, as it was over-run by Nazis. There was very little petrol and it was hard to move around. I had ceased to be an important hostess and led a lonely and quiet life. It was thus that Reinhard Henschel found me when he visited me on his way to take up a posting at the German Legation in Turkey. I used to go out shooting with our old chef, Yén, and when the villagers saw us seated side by side in the sleigh on our way to the coverts, they looked surprised. The Countess and the chef – a hint at the democratic times to come. They disapproved as they did not understand the concept of democracy believing it something wicked and suspect. I think they still think that and they are right.

At Devescer I had seen a certain amount of a former neighbour of ours in Bohemia, the Austrian Count, Zsiga Berchtold. Unlike many in our class, he was rather a good businessman, and he had managed to get enough petrol for his car. He frequently came over for dinner, and my chef, Yén, cooked us excellent dinners which we ate near the open fire in the big drawing room. We talked about the olden times and the times that were to come. We agreed that Tommy's behaviour with Louise de Vilmorin was unforgivable. Gradually he became more important in my life.

My first plan was to go to Turkey and Switzerland taking Bunny with me. This quite pleased Tommy as it meant that he would have Devescer to himself. As our lawyers began their discussions, he contemplated arranging a house for me in Totis, also in Hungary.

So our lawyers began their tedious discussions, which I am afraid continued for over a year. Tommy remained obsessed with Louise, and wrote her idiotic letters, declaring that he wanted to wake with the sunrays on them, tired and content. In one he said: 'Your Tim-Tim loves you with his heart, body and soul'. He was head over heels in love with her. This was not an easy phase for him. He was a bit scared of Hungarian society and how they would react to Louise as a separated wife of Pali, now possibly going about with him. He wanted to marry her. But it seemed that Pali was going about claiming that he was going to invite Louise back to Pudmerice and would remarry her, even though he had demanded a divorce from her in order to marry someone called, I think, Baroness Brunstetter.

By June 1943 legal wrangling between Tommy and me had reached a low ebb. He began to use Bunny as a weapon in this. He resented the implication that I was a good mother, which many of his friends told him, even suggesting we should be reunited as a pair. He threatened to cut my money off, saying I had an orchard that I could sell which would provide for me for years to come. At one point I suggested that I should continue to live in Devescer, but this he rejected. That summer he went to see Pali to have it out with him about his plans for Louise. There were none.

I do see that it was hard for Tommy. All he craved was to get to Louise. But the war, the impending divorce, and the impossibility of obtaining a German visa prevented this. Presently he bought me a small house with a park, which he put into Bunny's name.

My life was now more allied to Zsiga Berchtold, so I will save that for the next chapter. As with those phases when one marriage ends and another begins, there is sometimes an uncomfortable overlap. I will try not to confuse, or repeat, but my story with Tommy was coming to an end.

The divorce dragged on with more disputes. I had to give back the Majorat jewels,* and even then Tommy said that some were missing. But he told Louise that I was not 'as grabbing' – 'in details' as he had previously believed.

In March he prevented me from taking Bunny to Switzerland as the divorce was not settled and also because he believed it an unsafe time to travel. In Lausanne I stayed with friends for a short while. Then I went to Rome where I met Count Galeazzo Ciano and enjoyed a small 'walk-out' with him. I used to go along to visit him in his office in the Palazzo Venezia.

Ciano was Mussolini's Foreign Minister and also his son-in-law. He signed the 'Pact of Steel' with Germany in 1939 and restrained Mussolini from entering the war until the fall of France in 1940. In June 1942 Ciano had paid an important visit to Hungary to aid the process of returning to the Hungarians land that had been sequestered by the Romanians in the First World War. Though Ciano was married to Edda Mussolini, he often travelled without her. At a huge banquet given by the Hungarian Government in his honour, I remember being rather in love with him because he was attractive and had enormous charm.

Early in 1943 he had been appointed Ambassador to the Vatican. Our romance preceded a dramatic and terrible phase in Ciano's life. Early in 1943 he was planning the coup that finally overthrew Mussolini in July that year, and effectively ended Fascism in Italy. He then fled to Germany but was captured by pro-Mussolini partisans and Germans in Northern Italy. In 1944 he was tried for high treason, found guilty and executed.

I also enjoyed a 'walk-out' with Mario Panza, who used to come and stay with us when he was at the Embassy in Budapest. As I said, he was a great ladies' man.

On 19 March 1944 the Germans over-ran Hungary. By that time I was living with Zsiga in Budapest, and in April I packed up my belongings which I sent over to his town house. Tommy was

---

* Majorat jewels are those held in trust by primogeniture for the heir to the family.

not aware of the exact arrangements at the time, and I was a bit vague about them as he would have been less generous to me, but marriage to Zsiga was in the air. It was agreed the divorce would be heard in Veszprém.

Tommy kept Bunny with him at Devescer that summer on the grounds that he wished to keep her from being educated by me or falling under my influence. Honestly! So she amused herself by keeping fishes.

Later that summer I was gravely ill as I will explain in the next chapter. While in the sanatorium, I signed the divorce papers for Tommy, who found this an unsettling phase – as indeed it was. It had been two years since we broke contact and there had been many differences between us. He was such a kind man though and worried lest something should happen to me, partly for my sake and also for Bunny's. He was still under thrall to Louise, and she was uppermost in his thoughts. He wanted to marry her as soon as he was free. Because of the war, there was minimal contact between Louise and Tommy. I believe they spoke only three times on the telephone. I did not make any more difficulties but when I was better I went to see him in Budapest to resolve any outstanding matters, once again financial.

Tommy stayed on in Budapest until our divorce was finalised. He could not leave. First the Nazis prevented him from leaving. He was arrested by the Hungarian Nazis and put into prison, accused of high treason. Maybe this was because he had seen so many foreigners, even possibly because of his connection with Louise. They seized his assets and his bank accounts. He was kept on in prison even when, early in 1945, the Soviets liberated Hungary from the Nazis, putting it under strict Communist control.

The Russians seized all Tommy's estates, ransacking Pápa and throwing all the furniture out of the window. None of the fabulous collection from Versailles survived. They destroyed beautiful Devescer. Tommy could do nothing about it as he was in prison. He only escaped by bribing a former 'court jew' with the help of an interpreter. This man remembered Tommy and proved a true friend to him. But Tommy escaped with nothing left.

I suppose I should be grateful to Louise. She spared me from what would have been a dismal phase in my life.

POSTSCRIPT ON LOUISE DE VILMORIN
AND TOMMY ESTERHÁZY
by Hugo Vickers

Louise was living comfortably at Verrières near Paris. After the difficulties that overcame Tommy, he managed to make his way to Paris in order to claim Louise, with whom he had been obsessed for so long. He had found himself a job representing a commercial company, and he had what he called his 'life's plan' worked out. But the business side went gravely wrong when three of the team were arrested, and two more murdered by the Communists. This happened three weeks after his arrival in Paris. It put him in what he called 'a sort of void which weakened my standing.'

Tommy arrived at Louise's door from Hungary with nothing to his name. He was a dishevelled figure. Louise took one look at him announced: 'Un Esterházy n'est pas exportable!'

Later Tommy explained to her: 'Instead of quitting Paris the moment I saw I could not compete with the circumstances, who [sic] seemed to have their hand completely and firmly on you, I stayed in Paris and was a "wandering remorse" thus causing a continual agacement to you. Also I was vastly changed in some ways by the rather ghastly adventures and sufferings I was obliged to go through before I got free and arrived over the Hungarian frontier. I believe the only right thing to do, was that I should have left Paris and gone for a while until perhaps per chance things would have changed to the better.' [1] In fact he stayed on in Paris until some time in 1946.

The circumstances could not have been much worse. Louise had begun an affair with Duff Cooper, British Ambassador to Paris, on 8 November 1944. This went through the normal travails that any affair with Duff was bound to involve. In March 1946, he wrote to her to say that he loved her more than almost anyone in the world, and that he had not been unfaithful to her. He added: 'At the same time, as I have told you before, I don't and can't attach the same importance to physical fidelity as you do. I have never been faithful to anyone in that way and have never tried to be and if tonight I found a beautiful woman waiting in my bed I should not hesitate.' [2]

This was further complicated by Lady Diana Cooper, Duff's wife, falling for Louise. In July 1945 she wrote: 'You were sweet to write so quickly & say so convincingly that you love me. I love you dearly. I love no other woman. The one I loved (less than you) is dead. Let there be no mistake this is a love letter – not to be kept with Nellie de Vogué for it belongs to another category of areas.'[3] A few days later Lady Diana wrote again: 'I thought I was too old for a new love; you've taught me I was wrong for I love you.' [4]

But Tommy and Louise remained in touch. He forgave her for her cruelty in 1945: 'I do not now think you could help it, Louise.'[5] And he continued to maintain that although chances of marriage between them had been shattered, their 'loving friendship' remained 'unblemished.' [6]

In 1960 Tommy wrote to Louise of Bunny: 'She is grown up to be charming, not silly, quite pretty and also witty. So she will get on in life – I hope.' [7] And in 1961 he wrote, again of Bunny: 'I think you judge her too much on the same grounds as her mother is judged by. If you would meet her once without this prejudice, I am sure you would like her. And she is the nearest thing I have, fell and lone [sic] in my solitude.' [8]

When Etti finally married a very rich man, she was generous to Tommy and asked her husband to send him an allowance which he did. Tommy lived long enough to see Bunny married and to go to Scotland to meet his first grandchild. He died in Austria on 6 December 1964, at the age of 63.

SEVEN

Husband 4
Count Sigismund Berchtold, 1944-1949

Count Sigismund Alexander Leopold Corfitz Otto Tiburtius
Korsinus Heinrich von Berchtold (1900-79).
Born Buchlau, 14 April 1900.
Married (1) Ödenburg, 20 September 1944, Etti Wurmbrand.
Divorced 1949.
Married (2) 1953, Emilia Gostztonyi (1914-93). Divorced 1955.
(Twice married before that. She married fourthly, 1956 Prince
Vsevolode of Russia, divorced 1961).
Died Vienna, 20 July 1979.

I DID NOT actually marry my fourth husband, Zsiga Berchtold, until 20 September 1944, the civil marriage being regulated in Ödenburg, Hungary. But effectively I was his wife for some time before then. Zsiga was a distant cousin and also an old friend of mine. He persuaded me to marry him in order to have some protection during those war years. I accepted, but part of me hates to describe this as a real marriage for that reason. He was a good looking man, tall, and with a sense of humour. He could have been a good businessman, and in this I would encourage him.

Zsiga's full name was Sigismund Alexander Leopold Corfitz Otto Tiburtius Korsinus Heinrich von Berchtold, and he was the son of Count Leopold Berchtold, the Austro-Hungarian Minister of Foreign Affairs, the man who tricked the Emperor into declaring war on the Serbs by informing him, dishonestly, that

Serbian troops had already invaded Austro-Hungarian territory. The old Count had died in November 1942. The Berchtolds were amongst the richest and most ancient of the Magyár nobility. They had lovely estates at Pressing, where we could live in comfort. Zsiga's family had come from a beautiful renaissance castle in Moravia. As the second son, he had inherited the Hungarian properties.

I moved into his town palace in Budapest, eventually packing all my things at Devescer and moving them there in April 1944. It was easier to live in a city at this time, rather than a castle, and Zsiga could attend to his business. Life was quieter because of the war, and the increased activities of the Hungarian Nazis, but we still lived quite well, and I had not failed to bring my chef, Yén, with me from Devescer. We still saw a few friends, entertaining in a reduced way.

I was with Zsiga as Countess Berchtold, when in February 1944 I went to Ankara for three weeks, leaving Bunny with the Schulz family and their boys. The reason for this visit was to see my sister and her husband, Reinhard now being with the German Embassy in Ankara. I was aware that the war would not last much longer and wanted to establish some connections overseas. Reinhard was prominent in Turkish government circles.

Zsiga and I had intended to go there together but because of the military laws and as a well-known anti-Nazi he was denied an exit permit. The authorities were afraid that we might use the opportunity to leave the country for good. Through Reinhard's connections, I was allocated a seat on a German military plane flying via Vienna, Budapest and Istanbul once a week. The planes flew very low in those days for fear of enemy air attacks and after a bumpy flight, undertaken without my customary silk sheets, I arrived at Istanbul to be met by my brother-in-law. I missed the silk sheets in particular because bugs do not like them, and I knew that Turkish sleeping cars were full of these awful creatures.

As we were driving to town, Reinhard told me something that gave me a shock. At the instigation of the Nazis, Sophia had been forced to leave town, and he was expecting to be recalled. This came about because some members of the staff of the German Military Attaché had joined the Allies and one of them, a man called Erich Vermehren, was making speeches against Hitler from Egypt. The German Embassy in Ankara was in turmoil and the British press was suggesting that the next to defect would be the Henschels as they were well known for the anti-Nazi opinions. The logic was that as a member of an industrial family he would clearly be seeking safety abroad, and as an Austrian countess, she came from a family well-known for anti-Nazi sentiments.

Unfortunately these British press reports had the effect of bringing Reinhard's German anti-Nazi activities in Ankara to an end. This might have brought a swifter peace there. At the same time my sister was now in grave danger. She had never hidden her views which had been freely expressed in diplomatic circles. She had also spoken against Hitler at home in the presence of the Austrian nurse, who turned out to be the sister of an SS leader.

There was another reason for particular sensitivity at the German Embassy. The 'Cicero Affair' was in full swing – a spy stealing secret documents from the British Ambassador and selling them to the Germans. The German Embassy was terrified that the British Embassy would discover their spy and bring the whole plot to an end. So my visit was at a critical time. I later discovered that as my plane was taking me to Istanbul, Sophia was in a military plane heading to Vienna. Reinhard advised her not to go all the way to Vienna so she went to our house in Budapest.

From Istanbul I took the night train to Ankara, much missing my pink silk sheets. However, otherwise it was comfortable, and I was excited to be reaching Ankara. There I stayed in the comfortable Henschel house, a little way outside the town. There I found Sophia's three-year-old son, with the Nazi Austrian nurse, a Greek cook (who had formerly been at the British Embassy and still wore their livery), a Turkish maid and several dogs. Missing their mistress, the dogs came and slept on my bed. It was a strange situation as this German residence was next door to the house of the British attaché. Even though it was wartime, the British used to provide whisky for Henschel parties, and in exchange, the Henschels provided Rhine wine for British diplomatic dinner parties. But they never spoke to each other as this was strictly forbidden. The negotiations were conducted by the Greek and Turkish servants, who relished the situation. My brother-in-law warned me about all the servants. He said they were spying variously for the Allies, the Germans and the Turks.

Reinhard introduced me to Franz von Papen, the former German Chancellor and by then German Ambassador to Turkey. I expected to meet 'Satan in Top Hat' as he was dubbed by an American author, but to my surprise I found him a charming old gentleman. He loved Hungary and had been a great friend of Horthy, who had invited him regularly to the Hungarian State shooting parties. Papen was an expert on horse breeding and so we talked much about that. His wife was half-German, half-French and came from a well-known industrial family in the Saar district, the Boch-Galhaus. She spoke French without an accent. We often dined with the Papens, but made sure never to discuss politics.

Papen said he hoped my sister could soon return when things had cooled down in Berlin. He did say that unfortunately the Gestapo were now taking an interest in her case, and would certainly not let her cross the Bulgarian-Turkish frontier. Likewise, flying was impossible. But he was optimistic and said he would raise the matter with Hitler next time he went to Berlin. He expressed surprise that I had been allowed to travel as the Gestapo had said that on no account was 'Mrs Henschel's sister, Countess Esterházy' to be allowed to come to Turkey. I told him that I was now Countess Berchtold, and we laughed about this. Clearly the Gestapo had lost me in the name change. Papen said: 'Next time you might come as Countess Pálffy or Mrs Ryan, if you still have those passports.' I was not actually Countess Berchtold until the following September.

Papen and Reinhard introduced me to the Turkish Foreign

Minister, Numan Menemencioglu, a delightful international gentleman, then dexterously keeping Turkey neutral from the war. He said he missed Sophia in Turkey and would do all he could to get her back. He instructed the Turkish Ambassador in Berlin to intervene on her behalf.

One night the Papens gave a dinner party and invited a prominent German magician to entertain Numan. I had seen him before, as he was a rare, smart civilian on the plane that had brought me to Turkey. He performed many tricks, and at the end Numan asked him if perhaps there was one more piece of magic he could produce. Could he bring Mrs Henschel back to Turkey? The next day Papen sent another telegram about this to Berlin.

One evening at dinner at Reinhard's house, Numan took me aside and explained that the reason the Germans treated Turkey well was because they produced chromium which they needed to make steel for cannons and guns. They depended on those deliveries. That was why the Germans were so keen that they remained neutral and the Allies were equally keen to get them on their side. He said: 'We have a marvellous bargaining position, but only as long as the two sides are strong enough. If the Russian advance continues, Germany will be lost. For Turkey it is now time to revise her neutral position. I speak to you quite openly, dear Countess.' Then he added:

'I have received a telegram from Berlin this afternoon that Germany will occupy Hungary within the next few days. I would, if I may, rather advise you to return to your country – that is if you don't wish to stay abroad for good. You may tell this to your brother-in-law, who, I know, will not repeat it.'

That conversation was a considerable shock. I had come to Turkey not only to see my sister, but to plan for life in another country. I was to be overcome by events. Zsiga and Bunny were both in Hungary, and I had no money abroad. I would need some badly if I was to get them out. Nor did Reinhard have any funds overseas.

I consulted a few friends from neutral embassies, in particular

Baron Carl Hendrick Platen, the Swedish Chargé d'Affaires, who proved a particularly good friend. He understood our predicament only too well and said there was no alternative but to go home. Then a Greek diplomat, Jon Alexandre Djiras, another friend of Reinhard's, offered to get me a British passport from the British Embassy. But I had to get home. Zsiga, Bunny, and Sophia were in Budapest and my mother was in Vienna. The Nazis would have arrested all of them, and Bunny would have been given another name and placed in a Nazi camp. There was no shortage of evidence of anti-Nazi views in statements by my mother and sister.

So Reinhard took me by the night train to Istanbul and I returned on the German military plane. Zsiga was there to greet me when I arrived at Budapest.

My sister had still not been permitted to return to Turkey so she was living with us at our town house. As predicted by Numan, a mere two days after my return, on 20 March 1944, the Germans marched into Hungary. Their tanks rolled along our streets to be greeted by the Hungarian people with considerable apathy. Many turned their backs on them so as not to witness their arrival, though a few Hungarian Nazis in their green shirts received them with outstretched arms. I closed the shutters of our windows.

Two days after that, a field-grey German police car drove up outside our house. I watched them from the bathroom, one of the few windows without shutters. Two men in plain clothes jumped out and ran to the door. They rang the bell with fierce determination. 'Gestapo!' they shouted. 'Take us to Sophia Henshel.' The butler replied with much dignity, in his Hungarian German, that it was too early, that Mrs Henschel was having her breakfast in bed and that she was not yet ready to receive anybody. The men took out their pistols and pointed them at the butler, shouting: 'Take us instantly to her room!' He had to comply.

I watched what followed from my room on the other side of the hall. The butler knocked on Sophia's door saying: 'Frau Graefin?'

(the correct way of addressing her, as servants in Austria continued to call a married lady by the title of her childhood).

One of the Germans kicked the door open, pushed the butler out of the way and entered the room. My sister was still having breakfast in bed. He shouted at her: 'Gestapo! You are under arrest! Get dressed at once. You have to come with us!' The two men had the decency to turn their backs while Sophia dressed. Then they took her between them, rushed her downstairs, still with pistols in their hands, and out to their car. At this point one of the footmen appeared and opened the car door for Sophia. 'Does Frau Graefin have any orders?' he asked politely, but naively. 'NO!' shouted one of the Germans. At that moment dear old Yén appeared running out of the house. He gave my sister a glass jar of *pâté de faisan*, which she had always specially liked, and which only he could make so deliciously.

Off she went in the car, the two Gestapo men on either side of her. I sent a coded message to Reinhard as soon as we could. By then, as I learned later on, he had been giving orders to return to Germany. Fortunately Zsiga was not in the house when this arrest took place. He was in the country on some business matter. I dread to think what would have happened had he been there.

I went to the German Legation to protest but they were all violent Nazis. They would not, or perhaps could not, give me any information as to my sister's fate. In due course I was able to establish the bare facts – that my sister had been taken to a Berlin prison and then transferred to Ravensbrück Concentration Camp. When Reinhard returned to Berlin, he was interrogated by the Gestapo. Some months later, when we met in Vienna he told me that Sophia had been suspected of belonging to an anti-Nazi resistance group in Turkey. It was thought that like her husband she was preparing to join the Allies. Fortunately the Gestapo had no proof for this, though they were able to provide a list of violently anti-Hitler comments from her, most of them overheard and reported by the Austrian Nazi maid.

Sophia's case was submitted to Himmler. Due to Papen's

numerous well-intentioned interventions, it had become a matter of some importance in the Nazi regime. Himmler decided to lay it all before Hitler himself for him to decide. Baron Alexander von Dörnberg, a friend of ours, who was then Hitler's Chief of Protocol, was there when the reports were presented to Hitler. He read the insults that Sophia had delivered about him in Turkey. His face grew red, his hands began to tremble as he held the file, and finally he threw the entire file at the feet of his ADC and shouted: 'Keine Freilassung!' – No release! And so Sophia remained in the concentration camp until the end of the war.

That summer I fell gravely ill with high fever. I was in fact pregnant with Zsiga's child. The doctors found that one of my kidneys was affected by the tuberculosis from which I had suffered as a child. This disease had lain dormant in my body all those years. I had to have a life-saving operation to remove the kidney. This took place in Berlin at the height of the bombing. There were all these kind nurses looking after me as the bombs rained down. But I lost the baby.

Soon after that my divorce from Tommy came through. I married Zsiga a few weeks after the loss of my baby, but I think this had an unsettling effect on our marriage. It might have worked if the baby had lived. Men can tolerate anything but illness.

The political situation in Hungary was very distressing. The Germans had marched in, the Russians were advancing towards the Eastern frontiers, the Western Allies never came. Zsiga had a wonderful estate in the country and a beautiful castle, but it was practically worthless under the circumstances. One day we were at home there having lunch when some SS Officers arrived in search of rooms. Harriet Post, later the wife of Sumner Welles, was staying with us. She was married to a Hungarian before him. She was horrified. We asked the officers to lunch and if they had been planning to make problems, there were none that day.

Danger was never far away. When the Russians invaded Hungary, we decided we had to leave hurriedly. We just went, leaving behind us the horses and dogs and the nice people who worked for us. Zsiga obtained a special permit from the Germans saying he was on a special military mission. So he and I with Bunny left in his BMW car, which by some miracle he had been allowed to keep. We headed to Vienna. At the frontier the Germans inspected Zsiga's permit and then stood to attention to let us through. Our car was loaded to the top with luggage, but nobody inspected it. We stayed at the Hotel Imperial, where we had stayed so often before under happier circumstances.

Presently Yén and some other servants joined us there, arriving in a huge lorry filled with food reserves, which the hotel manager put in the cellars for us. Our valuables we kept in our rooms. We were not the first of our friends to leave Hungary. We found Vienna filled with both friends and relatives and every time we went into the streets there was someone we knew. We all shared the same aim – to reach Switzerland. Half of Hungary had been conquered by the Russians. It would not be long before we were in trouble again.

Bunny was also a problem for me. That December I sent her to Vaduz, where she spent Christmas with the Liechtenstein Royal Family. Then she went to Welda in Westphalia, Reinhard's country estate where she could be brought up with her cousin, Frederick. My mother went there too, arriving with only the clothes she wore since all her luggage had been stolen on the train journey, the very last train that ran and that could have taken her to safety. To lose the luggage was tiresome, but we were all alive, while many suffered worse fates.

During this operation of transfer I went via Berlin. While there my life was threatened, at a time when the British bombing was at its most intense. I was with a group of friends at the Hotel Bristol. There was Vinzi Windisch-Graetz, Martha Pronai, Missy Vassiltchikov, the Sapiehas and the Potockis. My mother was also there. A particularly fierce air raid began and we all retreated to the cellars. As Missy herself wrote: 'The noise was deafening - the crashes and tinkling of splintering glass never seemed to end.'

There have been many terrible stories about the fate of those who did not leave, not least Freddy Horstmann at Kerzendorf, his country estate in Germany. As I wrote earlier, he died of starvation in a Russian concentration camp.

We were still in Vienna, but aware of the need to escape. In order to get to Switzerland, we were told that the best route was across the frontier at Feldkirch, a tiny town in Western Austria. We were told that there was a high-ranking SS officer who could be bribed. This was encouraging news, as at that time, nobody was being allowed to leave. The Germans were saying that even women needed to stay behind to defend the Reich. I had the terrible vision that I might end up having to work in a German military hospital. Why would they make an exception for me, even as a Hungarian countess?

I went to Switzerland without Zsiga in the end. I paid the substantial bribe to the SS officer and it worked. At times like that it is a good idea to have some liquid funds at one's disposal if possible. I was allowed to go, but the officer forbade Zsiga to do so. He said that military rules prevented it absolutely. So Zsiga stayed and there was the hope that he could join me later.

I arrived in Switzerland, a free country – the freedom I had long dreamt of. I had made reservations at the Hotel Baur au Lac in Zurich and planned to go there immediately. I looked forward to seeing many friends. But no! I was placed in a Swiss refugee camp. That was a shock, and a nasty anti-climax after the euphoric moment of stepping onto Swiss soil. But I consoled myself that I was better off than my sister in a German concentration camp.

As it happened this miserable fate only lasted a few days. Influential friends contacted the Swiss authorities and I was released. The old pre-war life resumed with many invitations from friends who had stayed with us in Hungary in happier times. I spent some weeks in Swtizerland and Italy. In Rome I saw the Panzas and I also went to Florence. At one point I thought I became involved with Dino Philipson, and wondered if we had a future together, but it was not to be. He was an Italian politician, born around 1890, I suppose, who, had been a liberal democrat and a prominent anti-Fascist in his early days. When the Fascists took control, he was sent to Eboli, where he lived in a modest house, apparently a discreetly dressed, elegant figure, often sitting quietly in the Prince of Piedmont bar in the square.

He was close to Marshal Badoglio, another anti-Fascist, who was originally the conqueror of Abyssinia and later Chief of the General Staff. After Mussolini fell in September 1943, Badoglio formed a government and Dino became Under Secretary of State to the presidency of the council in Government. But when Rome fell to the Allies in June 1944, Badoglio surrendered to Eisenhower. Dino was in Switzerland when I was there, and later he served as Ambassador to OCDE. Meanwhile the war ended, my sister was set free and I visited her in Germany.

As for my husband, he stayed in Austria. He and his family had lost everything they had in Hungary and Czechoslovakia but he began to set up a new business career. He was quite successful. I admired his courage, but we spent most of the time apart. Effectively our marriage was over. Some years later, on 20 October 1949, we were divorced in Vienna.

Europe was not a happy place in those years after the war. The Russians were still there and many of us wondered if the peace would last. I relied on my sister and Reinhard at this time. Luckily their industrial enterprises were largely in the American zone of Germany, in Cassel. Reinhard still had his 18th century castle there, but he did not feel entirely safe. One day he received an offer from the Mexican government to go to Mexico and establish a branch enterprise of which he would be the head. He was to produce diesel engines and Henschel lorries there. My sister was delighted by this opportunity, her experience of Germany being in wartime, not to mention in the prisoner of war camp. So they prepared to set off.

Meanwhile I took Bunny to Switzerland and put her into the Marie José School in Gstaadt, where she was from 1945 to 1946. After that she was in Italy with Clara Fürstenberg, the mother of

Ira. At least she was contented and well fed, better than I could have looked after her.

As Austria was now a free state, and as my old Hungarian passport was only recognised in Franco's Spain, I applied and was granted Austrian nationality. I was anxious to start a new life, to visit various friends in America and start a career, anything to forget the bad moments of the war. So I applied for an immigration permit for the United States and after some endeavours, this was granted. I was one of the Austrian quota of immigrants. I wasted no further time. I sailed once more across the Atlantic to New York.

EIGHT

Husband No 5
Mr Deering Davis, 1949-1951

(William) Deering Davis (1897-19??)
Born Chicago, 20 March 1897.
Married (1) Devon, Pa, December 1926, Margaretta Barnwell
(Peggy) McNeal. Divorced ca. 1933.
Married (2) 10 October 1933, Louise Brooks (1906-85).
Divorced 1937.
Married (3) 1949, Etti Wurmbrand. Divorced Mexico, 1951.
Died 19??

I ARRIVED BACK in America, which I had last seen in 1934 when I sailed away from my unfortunate marriage to Clen Ryan. So much had happened in the meantime and yet scarcely fifteen years had passed. At that time I had been madly in love with Vladschi. In the years that had followed he had married a cousin of ours, a very pretty girl. They wanted a baby but no baby came. At that time a close friend of hers, the wife of an Italian diplomat found she was expecting a baby, but she was most anxious that her husband should not find out, since he had played no part in its conception. She was determined not to break up her family over this. So she and Vladschi's wife colluded to resolve their respective problems, keeping both husbands in sublime ignorance. The Italian lady retreated to a clinic to 'take a cure for her heart'. Vladschi's wife went to a clinic, and with the use of cushions, which grew bigger every week, feigned pregnancy. The baby was born, and swapped over.

Here Vladschi's wife made a mistake. She left the clinic too soon, arriving home too suspiciously fit and well after her supposed confinement. At first Vladschi received her home and was delighted with the baby. Then he grew suspicious. Friends told him it was bigger than it should have been. Questions were asked at the clinic and the dreadful truth emerged. I thought it was rather a curious story, touching in a way. Everybody was acting with the best intentions and there was no need for either of the husbands to have known the truth. The two mothers only wanted the best for them. I felt sorry for them, but especially sorry for Vladschi.

I arrived in the new world with as little money as when I left it. As I sailed past the Statue of Liberty I wondered if this would be the land of freedom – freedom from fear as Eleanor Roosevelt kept promising. There were no rose filled barges, or Rolls-Royces to greet me this time, but I was back in America. I had to queue up with the other Austrian immigrants to get in, and was asked a hundred questions. 'Was I a Nazi?' 'No.' 'Did I belong to the SS?' 'No, only men did', I said. 'Was I a member of any other criminal organisations?' 'No.' 'Was it my intention by coming to the United States to murder the President?' Honestly! I laughed. The immigration officer did not laugh. But eventually that boredom passed and I was in.

I was met by friends who took me to New York. I thought back to poor Clen. He had spoiled me so, in his way, and far too much. I had been too young to appreciate it. I confess he had bored me, and that is a word one should forget, and which is used too frequently and too easily. I checked into the St Moritz Hotel on Central Park South.

Next morning I got out my old address book, a gift from Clen that had survived from that marriage and made its way through the war, and started to ring up the numerous friends, whose names were written in it. Some had died, others had disappeared, some had moved, but I was able to speak to a good number of them. Many invited me, with that legendary hospitality that

Americans possess, and soon my appointments diary was filling up nicely.

I did need a job, however. So I went to see Herr Matschler, the Austrian Consul-General. He was most helpful. He pointed out that all Americans had a job, and that everyone seemed to be in a hurry. The streets of Manhattan were filled with people rushing along, in a hurry, all very busy or pretending to be. In Austria and Hungary it was not like that. I never saw Pali or Tommy or even Zsiga in a hurry. Herr Matschler, a nice old gentleman, paused for a moment and then said: 'Why don't you come and work here at the Consulate General? We need someone like you. We are rather isolated and you could help us with our public relations.' I had no idea what public relations was or were, but I accepted. As I was leaving, he added: 'Don't forget, never be in a hurry! You don't have to come in sharp on time, but whenever it suits you.' So, for the first time in my life, I had a job.

This was in fact the first of three jobs in quick succession. My second job was working for Gayelord Hauser, the great dietician. He was the man more responsible than any other for introducing the natural food cult and his book, *Look Younger, Live Longer* was a world best seller, and translated into more than forty languages. He was a proponent of warm baths, herbal teas, and recommended a diet of fruit juices and vegetable soups. This brought him many admirers in the world of film, particularly Greta Garbo and Marlene Dietrich. He formed his theory when he had serious tuberculosis in Switzerland and a monk told him that he would die if he continued to eat dead foods. 'Living foods make a living body,' he said. He changed his diet, survived and went on to recommend similar ideas to the world.

Gayelord could be very funny. He had a special theory about weight. He said once: 'I tell wives that if they want to know their correct weight, they should put on their wedding dresses. If their husbands laugh, then I advise the wives to make the husbands put on *their* wedding suits.'

I also worked for Elizabeth Arden at the time when she was

promoting her wonderful eight-hour cream.

I was thirty-five years old and I had already been married and divorced four times. I preferred to be in the married state.

I am often asked about my fifth husband, and really I can remember very little about him. I spent my time with old friends and some new acquaintances. Among the latter was a nice middle-aged man, who, I soon noticed, took a greater interest in me than others. He took me out quite often, or as they say in America, he 'courted' me. There was nothing special or unusual about him, and he was no aristocrat. But we were living in democratic times, and I did not mind a shot at being democratic. I do not like to live alone, and I particularly did not like living alone in New York, where I still felt a little lost. So when he announced: 'I love you, would you marry me?' I said: 'Yes, why not?'

He was an American from Chicago, called Deering Davis. We were married in the late autumn of 1949 in Chicago. Deering was an interior decorator, working for the Studio of Interior Design, Frederick & Nelson. We met in New York and he was set to marry me. He used to say that while he was working the time passed quickly but after five o'clock in the evening time seemed endless. I think he envied me the many friends I had, who helped to keep me busy. I am not at all sure that I should have married him. Actually, it was a terrible mistake as it did not work at all.

It is funny that it is only now that I learn more about him, this shadowy figure who was briefly a part of my life. Apparently the Davises were a well-known family. They were of Welsh stock originally and came over to the USA in 1640. Deering's grandfather was born in New York and went to Chicago with William Deering and Cyrus McCormick. They founded the International Harvester Company. His father, Dr Nathan Smith Davis II (1858-1920), a Methodist physician, founded the Chicago Medical Society and had a house on the site of today's Marshall Field Store. He married Jessie Bradley Hopkins, a Colonial Dame, who was born in Madison, Wisconsin. She was the daughter of James C. Hopkins, a judge of the U.S. Court, who came from New England. Deering's full name was William Deering Davis, after his grandfather's partner and he was born, the youngest of four, on 20 March 1897.

Another thing I didn't know about Deering was that he had been married to the silent film star, Louise Brooks. She was famous for about five years in the 1920s and the rest of her life was a long decline. Some say she was one of the finest film stars of the silent era, and her most famous film was Pabst's adaptation of a Wedekind play, *Pandora's Box*, in which she played a free-living girl who destroyed a succession of men before succumbing to Jack the Ripper. She also made the sensational film, *The Diary of a Lost Girl*, but in the middle of her life was reduced to being a sales assistant at Saks, Fifth Avenue. Towards the end, she was rediscovered by Kenneth Tynan and has taken her place amongst the immortals.

Louise Brooks met Deering in Chicago in July 1933. She was on the rebound from a relationship and was short of money. He was then known as something of a playboy, a society bachelor and a polo player, who had spent some time in Paris. He was also a good dancer. As it happens he was no bachelor since he had recently been divorced from a Philadelphia socialite horsewoman called Peggy McNeal. At any rate Louise Brooks married Deering in October 1933 and the two of them made plans for a dance act. First they travelled together on a prolonged honeymoon, and then they returned to Chicago and launched their dance team at Chez Paree in February 1934. The cream of Chicago society gathered to watch them dance, and they went through an adagio, a rhumba and later an apache dance. They danced together for a month at the Chez Paree. Then, a week after their stint was over, Louise left town. She departed by train without a word to Deering in March 1934, leaving only a note of her plans. Evidently she thought him just a legal nuisance and left without asking for a dime of alimony. They were divorced in 1937.

Some years had passed before Deering met me. Immediately

after the marriage, boredom set in. From the moment we were married, he stopped taking me out. There was no more 'courting'. He said he preferred a light American dinner, some Hamburgers and deep-frozen vegetables at home rather than spending a lot of money in restaurants. He cooked dinner himself, the result corresponding to my worst expectations. Generally I refused to touch the food, at which point he took offence and went straight to bed. I soon realised that things could not go on like that.

As far as this marriage was concerned I had made a grave mistake. The first time I married I had been violently in love with another man. This time I had agreed to marry in order to have somebody with me. Now I did have him with me – and far too much. What could be done? I could not just kill him. If I asked for a divorce, he would refuse, as there were no other women, nor even men in his life. I thought, and thought . . .

As so often in life, luck came to my rescue. One day, about two months after the marriage, he suggested he would cook me a 'delicious lunch' in our 'sweet little apartment'. I replied: 'Why don't we just have a light lunch at the Oyster Bar in the Plaza?'

'Very expensive,' he replied, but he agreed, as a special favour, that he would be there at 1pm. I realised that he had taken offence again, but I did not care. I booked a table and went to the Plaza, arriving there on the dot of one. Deering was usually most punctual, yet by 1.15 there was no sign of him. I started to order.

'Don't you prefer to wait for the gentleman?' enquired the head waiter.

'No,' I replied, and enjoyed an excellent light lunch.

When I had finished, Deering still had not come. I paid the bill with the wages for my work, and left. On returning to the apartment, I discovered that my husband's modest possessions, a few ready-made suits, some shirts and a cheap volcano-fibre suitcase were no longer there. He had left. There was no message, nothing. In fact he had gone forever, and I never ever heard from him again. It was the best solution. I was free again.

I was then living in a modest hotel, where I hired a very small room. Cecilia Sternberg came to see me and left an amusing account of the visit in her book, *The Journey*. She asked me what had happened to Mr Deering Davis, and I told her: 'He's gone. It was only a temporary arrangement.' She remembered that I then smiled and said: 'Perhaps he didn't like sleeping in the cupboard.' I opened a large clothes cupboard in which, besides a lot of my clothes, there was a sort of camp bed, which came down from the wall when needed in the night. She was rather surprised, I think.

I cooked for her, a new skill for me, and we talked about the future. I had to stay in New York to get my divorce. It was always such a bore getting these divorces. Somehow they took such a long time to come through. This one was arranged for me by the kind Austrian Consulate. It finally took place in Mexico in 1951. Meanwhile my friends gathered round and gave me what they called a consolation party for 'poor Etti'. Some years later I heard that Deering had died.

That is all I can say about Deering Davis.

Cecilia Sternberg was again surprised when I told her that I would remarry once more, as soon as my divorce came through. She thought that I did not take marriage that seriously on account of my first love for Vladschi those many years before. She may have had a point, because certainly I did not want to suffer again as I had over Vladschi. Therefore there was always perhaps a certain reserve, which made it easier for me to face the frequently changing circumstances of my life.

In 1950, a little time after this fifth marriage came to a sudden end, I sent for Bunny. She came to America where she lived with a family in Detroit and I never saw her. By this time my sister and Reinhard were living happily in Mexico. Still in New York I sat next to Nelson Rockefeller (later Vice-President of the United States) at dinner. He was a friend from the Clen Ryan days. I liked him and his wife. I had always valued his advice, even if I had not always taken it. I like being given advice by healthy, tough men.

Nelson said to me: 'If I were you, I would not stay in the United States. Here you need a lot of money to live in the style you were used to in Europe. Why not go south to Latin America? I know those countries pretty well. They have a great future, and you can live there very agreeably on not so much money.' He told me he had substantial investments in Venezuela and promised me some introductions in various Latin American countries. Next morning his chauffeur came round to deliver these.

I am the kind of person who acts on an idea when it seizes my imagination. I did not wait long. First I sent Bunny and my mother to Chile together. Bunny lived mainly with my mother and went to a very good school there, soon learning to speak some Spanish. I was soon sending them a telegram to let them know I was joining them. I flew to Santiago. I was thrilled to see them again.

There now began a happy drifting phase in my life. I felt secure to be away from Europe at that troubled time, and glad to have all my immediate family nearby.

I used to go out a lot and I loved to dance. Nelson Rockefeller had given me an introduction to a wonderful man called Baron Nicky Nagel. He was a German landowner, settled in Chile. I went to see him the morning after my arrival, bearing Nelson's letter. 'How funny,' he said. 'You, an Austro-Hungarian being introduced to a German-Chilean by an American. That is a good omen for the friendship between the various partners.'

Nicky was a gentle and courteous man, and we all loved him. He was very generous and paid for Bunny's schooling. He taught her how to drive. He invited us all to stay at his large house on a hill overlooking Santiago, near the famous Miraflores golf course. His outward appearance was of the Pali Pálffy type. Unlike Pali, he was a good businessman and one of the biggest sheep breeders in South America. He had built up the herd himself and was selling the wool at most advantageous prices. He followed the markets closely himself, and was adept at judging them.

Unfortunately he had a wife, a Swiss from a large banking family in Basle. He had been married to her for a long time, and being an honourable man, he was intensely loyal to her. I know that he fell for me and in turn I fell for him. He used to go on inspection journeys to visit his large estates in the country. He used to take me with him and we rode on horseback. It reminded me of my country life in Moravia, Slovakia and Hungary. I loved the Chilean landscape, its mountains, volcanoes and lakes. The people we visited were so hospitable. Some had lovely houses, mostly in the Spanish style with large verandahs to keep off the heat and sun in the summer. There were flower-filled central courtyards filled with delicious perfumes, and often with nesting birds.

To return to Santiago was always to feel a little sad. Here again was town life, civilization, and as in New York the dinner parties and cocktail parties. The diplomatic corps were again at the centre of all this, so it was somewhat similar. The inspection tours began to become more frequent and to include the stud farms which had huge appeal to me. And so I fell more and more for Nicky, considering him my great love. But I was aware that his Swiss wife was becoming upset by these rural excursions. It was understandable. Nicky would always stand by her, and not being a Louise de Vilmorin, I had no desire to break up his marriage. Sooner or later I would have to disappear. Nicky became desperate, and so did I. Finally I booked a plane for Lima. We had a tearful parting at the airport. I promised to come back again soon, but as so often happens in situations like that, I never did. I did not see him again, but my stay in Chile with Nicky was like a dream.

In Lima I stayed but a short while as I wanted to get to my sister in Mexico. While there, however, I stayed with my Polish friends, Georg and Susanita Potocki, who had escaped there before Poland was occupied by the Germans and had thus been able to transfer their funds there. They lived in a beautiful house with a lovely garden. The moist climate in Peru was such that flowers and plants grow easily. The Potockis were the kindest of hosts. On I went to Mexico.

The Henschels were there to greet me. As I said before,

Reinhard was working there with the family firm, run by his elder brother. They loved Mexico and had settled happily there after their travails in Turkey and Europe. They fetched me from the airport and drove me to their lovely house in Chapultepec. Frederick, their son, was at a Jesuit school and had learned a lot of Spanish. He spoke this without an accent. He was such a nice boy, with a good sense of humour and the inherited intelligence of a Baltazzi. I soon felt at home there and spent many hours talking with my sister as we had so much to catch up on.

The Henschels had many friends there, and I soon met these. There were a number from Europe, mostly from France. Dick de la Rosière handled European private funds, was a passionate golfer and a great shot. He understood all the complicated intricacies of Mexican business. The Henschels introduced me to Bill O'Dwyer, the American Ambassador, who had previously been Mayor of New York. He was a wild Irishman, always ready for fun. When in New York, he had resigned when a police scandal was unraveled, ironically with my first husband, Clendenin Ryan, hot on his heels. President Truman had appointed him Ambassador to Mexico in 1951 but soon after that he had been obliged to return to the States to answer questions about organized crime figures. Nothing was proved against him, but the rumours hung about him. When I met him, he was about to give up his job and go into business as an international lawyer, using his political and diplomatic connections to make a success of it. Unfortunately he had a tendency to drink very heavily. One evening he took me to dinner at the 1,2,3 and suddenly proposed marriage. I employed the usual kind method of not hurting his feelings by thanking him and saying I would think it over. The subject was never raised again, and we remained friends.

These Latin men! There was another who wanted to marry me – Manuel Reachi, a great Mexican film producer, highly successful in business, though what business he would never define and I never found out. That was the way with Mexican businessmen – they plunged into whatever business appealed to them. Manuel had an extraordinary super-modern house in the famous resort of Cuernavaca, half way between Mexico City and the Pacific Coast. It was built around a huge swimming pool, and no doubt many deals were settled as Manuel and his colleagues lay around the pool.

He was middle-aged and of Lebanese descent, very good looking and attractive. But I hate to say it he gave me the impression of being something of a gangster! Women loved him. He was surrounded by Mexican girls from the world of the cinema. Manuel had been married several times. One wife was Agnes Ayres, the celebrated silent star so memorably carried off by Rudolf Valentino in *The Sheik* (1927). Then he married a Mexican socialite, Carmen Lopez Figueroa, and then the lady whom I knew later as Rosemarie Kanzler, when she lived on Cap Ferrat in the South of France. I will have something to say about her later. His most recent wife was a German actress called Hilda Kreuger. He kept her under firm control or so he thought. I was shocked when he revealed his methods. Whenever she left, even on a short trip, he demanded that she hand over all the jewels he had given her. Only when she returned did he let her have them back. 'That always makes her come back,' he said with a canny understanding of her nature. But one day she left suddenly, taking a huge diamond ring with her. He sent his 'pistoliers' after her – his bodyguards – but they were too late at the airport and she had flown away. Later she asked for a divorce and got it. Manuel related this story with increasing rage as he told it. I thought it quite amusing.

One day he too asked me for marriage. But I was extremely wary, put off by the many stories I had heard. This time I did not even hesitate, I said 'No' right out. He was not offended. He was not disappointed. He was a realist. He just said that he would look for someone else.

The Henschels also had a summer house in Cuernavaca, with a big swimming pool. We invariably spent our weekends there.

Another figure who appeared, rather more serious than Manuel, was Bruno Pagliai, an Italian self-made man who had retreated to Mexico during the war. He worked hard and possessed the necessary shrewdness to cope with Mexican vagaries in business. He had risen to be an important industrialist. He told me that twice already he had made and lost his fortune, but he never gave up, and presently success came for a third time. He ran the huge Tube-Plant which he controlled 100 per cent. He was alert to the fact that the Mexican oil industry would presently need steel tubes and he was there to provide them.

He worked hard, but he played hard too. While I was there he was married to his second wife, a beautiful girl from the Guirola family, a great coffee growing family from El Salvador. Later he divorced her and in 1957 he married the famous film star, Merle Oberon. He had an enormous town house on the hills above Mexico City and a beautiful ancient house from the Spanish era, again in Cuernavaca. There he and his wife lived very informally.

Also in Mexico was Prince Max Hohenlohe, a lazy man who never took life too seriously. He was full of ideas but none ever seemed to materialize. He was always in a good mood, cheerful and amusing. I had known him since childhood days in Moravia and Bohemia. He had owned a famous castle, Rothenhaus, in the Sudeten, but this was now lost to the Czechoslovak Communists. He often came over to the Henschels.

Max or Mapl, as he was known, was married to Piedita Yturbe, from the well-known Spanish-Mexican family, which had owned huge estates in Mexico before the Mexican Revolution of 1916. Like our estates in Bohemia, these had been confiscated, leaving only the 'cascos', their former residence on the hacienda. Mapl took us to the casco at Hacienda de San Miguel, a huge seventeenth century building which had been able to accommodate 200-300 guests with no problem. It was sad to see it so run-down. We concluded that very often private owners looked after their properties better than the huge state-owned agglomerates under their often lazy and corrupt administrators.

Mapl often spoke of fantastic deals that he was about to start up with the Mexican President or Finance Minister. We could never get any facts about these, and I fear many were just hot air.

But some deals did work. In Cuernavaca he used to buy plots of land and build modest houses on them with the help of an architect friend. An American girlfriend advised him sensibly as to exactly the kind of house an American would want, and she got it just right. Another American decorated the interior quite extravagantly, and Mapl moved in for a time. Then he put it on the market as 'a former princely residence.' This worked wonderfully for him and he was forever moving house as a result. Then he had a transaction going in Spain, and this grew to become a huge success, really more by luck than anything else. Reinhard had a cousin called Duckwitz who had been at the German Embassy in Madrid. He lost his job when the Embassy was closed down and went with his wife to a sleepy fisherman's town as a cheap place to live while they looked to the future. The place they found was Marbella, a distinctly dull place, but Duckwitz supplemented his meagre income by buying and selling small plots of land. Mapl and his son, Alfonso, heard about this and wanted somewhere to build a house for later on, having lost his estate in Bohemia. The price was ridiculously low, just a few centavos per square metre. He never thought of developing it, the house was just for himself, but it proved a fantastic investment. Alfonso turned Marbella into a famous club, shocked the world by marrying Ira von Fürstenberg when she was only 15, and the Costa del Sol became a renowned retreat for summer holidays.

My visit came to an end. Reinhard and Sophia took me to Acapulco. I did not care for it, considering its natural beauty had already been destroyed by extravagant building. But Frederick, their son, and I went fishing in the Pacific together, sometimes perhaps going out a little too far for safety.

But I was getting restless again. Much as I loved Latin America, and particularly Mexico, I began to yearn for Europe. Friends were writing frequently that the state of Europe was improving and how optimistic they were. Europe was my home, and I longed to go home, even if I did not have an actual home to go to. Bunny was still at school in Chile. Should I stay, would we all just merge into South American life and never be seen or heard of again?

Bunny needed to complete her education in more sophisticated surroundings. Though her father, Tommy Esterházy, had lost all his worldly goods and was now living quietly in Geneva, she deserved a better chance in life. I did not want her to grow up and marry a South American. My mother, also in Chile, was still my responsibility.

Our life in South America had been an interesting phase and a good way of life, but it could not last. We were running out of money. I needed to take a grip of things. I felt that the time had come to return to Europe and see what kind of future I could create for us there.

I was sad to leave but once again I sailed away. I made my way to France.

NINE

Interlude: A Biographical Note
Dr Arpad Plesch, 1889-1974

by Hugo Vickers

W e are about to meet Dr Arpad Plesch, Etti's sixth and last husband. As editor, I promised to intervene as little as possible in Etti's story. However, since Dr Plesch's story is such an intriguing one, and since he had lived his life in parallel to Etti's but in a different milieu, it is helpful to have a biographical note on him at this point. These are therefore the results of my own researches with the help of FBI papers as well as notes made by Arpad Plesch himself. Etti's narrative resumes in Chapter Ten.

Etti's marriage to Arpad Plesch was the culmination of an extraordinary marital career for her, and would not have been possible but for the political and social changes that had occurred as the result of two world wars. It was a union of her aristocratic roots with his enormous commercial fortune. Thus it was of benefit to both parties, and the combination worked well. The superficial facts are that it was the marriage of an Austro-Hungarian countess with a self-made Jewish businessman of humble origins. But it was more than that. Here was a woman of the world allying herself to an extremely intelligent and versatile international financier, whose brain could encompass any topic. There were many prejudices against him, but there is plenty of testimony to his erudition and to what good company he was.

Perhaps because he was so rich and because some of his actions were such that they caused intense suspicion, Arpad Plesch's movements were closely monitored, especially during the Second World War. There are pages of files on him at the FBI, some of which have been released and there are further reports lodged in the National Archives in Washington. FBI reports exist on many public figures. It says something for Plesch that despite the numerous unpleasant allegations made against him, and despite the restrictions imposed on his travels during wartime, nothing was ever proved against him.

Etti said little about Arpad Plesch's origins other than that his fortune came from sugar plantations in Haiti. She described him as a Hungarian lawyer, who made some wise investments, not least in the lucrative Societé des Bains de Mer in Monte Carlo.

He was in fact a distinguished lawyer and economist, an international financier and a collector of rare botanical books. He was a keen yachtsman. Later he had a good boat, on which it was possible to spend a night, and where the food was delicious. After the war, he was one of the first to invest in Japanese industry at a time when there was general antipathy to all things Japanese.

Etti noted that he travelled on a Haitian passport and that this made their travelling very difficult. He needed a visa everywhere he went, even if he crossed the border to San Remo. We will read her version in Chapter Ten.

Arpad Plesch was born in Budapest on 25 March 1889, the youngest son of Ludwig Plesch, a businessman, and Honoria Seligman. According to his elder brother, John Plesch, both sides of the family had wandered from Bohemia into Hungary. His mother's family came from Alt-Ofen near Budapest. His maternal great-great uncle, Moses Spitzer, had sailed round the world three times. Another maternal ancestral uncle had gone to England and changed his name from Loewi to Lion and sired Nelson's celebrated paramour, Emma, Lady Hamilton. John Plesch related that his Plesch great-grandfather had been a successful brewer, who established the first Lodge of Freemasons in Hungary. There was even an inn called 'The Good Old Plesch'.[1]

John Plesch (1878-1957) became a scholar and physician and a friend of Einstein. His interests extended from science to politics, from the stage to art and music. Of the early life of the Plesches, Susan George, Arpad's niece by marriage, recalled:

'The Plesch family in Budapest was extremely poor. There were three sons and a daughter, the sons were: Matyas, Janos [John] and Arpad. The girl was Mirza. They were my father's first patients and he treated them for nothing because they could not afford to pay. Mirza always told me that the boys could sleep in one bed, but she, as a girl, slept most of the time on the floor.'2

Susan George liked Arpad:

'Arpad was a charming, polite man, incredibly astute and wordly. He was greatly interested in botany, wrote several books on the subject and loved his beautiful flowers and fruit trees in Beaulieu-sur-Mer, in the South of France. He was a most devoted brother to Mirza, whom he loved deeply. Actually, he adopted and educated Mirza's oldest son, Egon, who became a psychiatrist in London [in 1933].'3

The young Arpad went to college in Budapest. According to a report filed in the FBI, he was 'of firm build, with straight black hair and black eyes'. He had 'a swarthy complexion, clean shaven, with no marks or scars.' He spoke French, German, Italian, Magyár, and several other European languages. His English was good and delivered 'in a deliberate manner with great precision.' His FBI report also stated: 'His manner is suave, self-assured and distinctly continental in dress and deportment and he is said to have one of the shrewdest financial and legal minds in the world.'4

Plesch was educated at the universities of Budapest, Paris, Oxford and Berlin, receiving several scholarships. He became a Doctor of Laws in 1911. He wrote a biography of Adolphe Quetelet, the Belgian scientist, known for his study of man and the development of his faculties, and for his work on anthropometry, and he published several legal studies. The Hungarian Ministry of Education sent him to the London School of Economics in 1913. He received the legal diploma of barrister and judge in 1925.

At the beginning of the war he was mobilised, serving as a Captain in the Royal Hungarian Army. He was wounded in 1914, won two medals for bravery and later served in the economic section of the Austro-Hungarian War Office.

In 1918 they sent him to Vienna, where, in 1919, all the Successor States of the former Austro-Hungarian Empire gave him the mission of liquidating the economic representations of Austria-Hungary in Stockholm and Zurich. He became First Secretary in Vienna in 1920, and in Berlin in 1920.

In 1923 he retired from the diplomatic service in order to devote himself to financial and investment interests. Later he would cite the reason for this as having inherited a considerable fortune from one of his uncles, thus needing to devote time to nurturing this. Mirza told her daughter-in-law that Arpad became 'adjutant/secretary to the Polish Finance Minister during the First World War and stayed in his employ'.5

This finance minister was Michal Ulam, a landowner, architect and international building contractor. Originally he came from Lemberg, the capital of Galicia in Austria-Hungary, and was the uncle of S.M. Ulam (1909-1984), one of the world's most famous mathematicians, sometimes described as 'the father of the H-Bomb'. Michal's wife, Leonina (sometimes Leonie) Caro was born in Erfurt, Germany on 27 May 1883 and descended from a famous 15th century scholar in Prague. The Ulams had a family saying – much repeated: 'Reich sein ist nicht genug, man musst auch Geld in der Schweiz haben' – 'It is not enough to be rich, one must also have money in Switzerland.'6

When Plesch was first associated with the Ulams, the three used to go to St Moritz where, because they were Jewish, the other holiday-makers crossed the road to avoid them.

Plesch had a long clandestine affair with Leonie Ulam which began in 1920. In FBI files dating from 1941, by which time Leonie had married Plesch, she was described as 'large and fleshy, a gaudy dresser, and uses heavy make-up'. Etti's daughter recalled her as 'rather the Helena Rubinstein type'.7 The FBI further stated: 'His former mistress, now his wife, is reputed to be one of the wealthiest women in Central Europe, and it is believed that she gave him his financial start.'8 This fortune was always said to have come from having been the mistress of Bela Kuhn (briefly the dictator of Hungary during the White Terror of 1919). Kuhn was said to have stolen Hungary's gold reserves and these she had acquired from him. True or false, there was no shortage of money.

There was one Ulam daughter called Marysia, born just before 1918. Her involvement in this saga was odd (of which more later). So too was Plesch's involvement with the Ulam family.

Plesch's financial career developed swiftly. Following the marriage (in 1933) of his brother John to Melanie Gans, whose family were worth over 50 million marks, Plesch decided that as he was the financial brains of the family, he should manage the family's business affairs. He became principal shareholder of Chemische Fabrik Grieshelm Elektron (which belonged to his sister-in-law), and through the merger of various companies, he became a member of the board of the new I.G. Farben in Frankfurt in 1925. This was later to be damaging to him since I.G. Farben was the company that manufactured Zyklon B, the gas used in the gas chambers of the Holocaust. Although he claimed he had been in dispute with the company and was not involved with them after 1932, there were allegations that he was an intermediary when the Germans did not want their Swiss business implicated in post-war Holocaust investigations.

From 1920 until 1930 Plesch lived in Berlin, at a time when there was much foreign investing in Germany, particularly by the English and American, while Germany was in its period of economic reconstruction. In 1929 he created the Stiftung Arpad Plesch in Switzerland to hold his extensive investments. The following year he moved to Paris at a time when other Plesches were also on the move. His brother, Professor John Plesch had become a successful physician and, as we have seen, had married into the von Gans family, owners of one of the companies that merged to form I.G. Farben. Now a rich man, he left Germany for London in 1933, bringing with him his three children. Susan George knew the doctor well:

> 'I loved Janos [John], a fascinating man. I am not convinced how good a doctor he was (some say he was a charlatan), but he 'sounded' good. A great connoisseur of art and music, wonderful conversationalist and yet, happiest when he could eat Mirza's, his sister's, mashed sardines with butter and lemon in her kitchen!'9

John Plesch's memoirs were described as 'almost a Who's Who of Central European science, culture, and politics in the two generations preceding the Second World War.'10 He claimed that as a doctor, 'his greatest pleasure must be the sight of the healthy person whom he has cured. The more a doctor hates sickness the livelier will be his ambition to get rid of it, and the more elementary will be his urge to heal.'11 He was full of theories, one of which was: 'Homosexuality in human beings is a sign of exhaustion in the generative forces of the human seed,'12 which was followed by some extraordinary comparisons even in the political arena: 'Recall the pictures of that virile bull Mussolini addressing his followers; his arms are outspread vigorously as though he would like to grasp the whole world. And compare him to that asexual rice-pudding vegetarian Adolf Hitler, who wouldn't raise his arm properly even to execute the gesture named after him, but who just feebly raised his underarm in reply.'13

John Plesch bought a house near Aylesbury and set himself up as a doctor in a penthouse in Park Lane without going through the accepted British training process. He was one of those fashionable doctors, with curious, unconventional methods, who enjoyed an extraordinary success with the patients he secured in London society. The economist, Maynard Keynes described him as 'something between a genius and a quack' but reckoned that he saved his life by administering Prontosil at a time when British doctors despaired of him. When he cured Einstein of pericarditus by prescribing bed rest, a salt-free diet and diuretics, Einstein remarked: 'He is a swine, but he's my friend.'[14]

Dame Frances Campbell-Preston wrote: 'a certain section of society flocked to him with real or imaginary illnesses.'[15] One such was her mother, Mrs Arthur Grenfell. Two diagnoses emerged from the Professor to reduce Frances's excess teenage weight. He told Mrs Grenfell that he had noticed that ancient statues in Italy often had their contours worn away by exposure to the elements. He prescribed that she should be hosed down and then rubbed with a horse brush. When this had no effect, he recommended that she ran round Hyde Park in a little vest. Frances's father vetoed this on grounds of decency.

When Mrs Grenfell had a bad cold, he urged an extremely hot bath, and that she be put to bed without being dried, blankets heaped on top of her, and then washed in vinegar. More seriously he almost killed John Buchan (Lord Tweedsmuir) by suggesting that because his false teeth did not fit properly, air was filtered through them and ulcers resulted. He recommended insulin 'with near fatal results'.[16]

Dr Plesch was the author of another book, a rather curious one. *Rembrandts within Rembrandts* (1953) was a controversial attempt to discover hidden faces concealed within Rembrandt's paintings and drawings. As with many of his activities, its contents gave rise to much lively discussion amongst experts and other interested parties.

In about 1937 Arpad Plesch found himself under arrest in London, and remanded in gaol. At the behest of John, Mrs Grenfell spent almost an entire day on the telephone assuring everybody that he was innocent. According to her daughter:

> I am not sure she even enquired what the charge was, but I do remember her pursuing the Home Secretary [Sir Samuel Hoare] relentlessly, and ringing a good many prison governors in the hope of finding which prison he was in and telling them to let him out. I don't remember if he was charged in the end, or found guilty. Typically, as a teenager, I lost interest. We weren't totally innocent of hoping all Plesches might be arrested.[17]

In 1936 Arpad Plesch became involved in the celebrated law case for which he is particularly remembered. He had long believed that gold was the best 'hedge' against inflation and the danger of devaluations. In the 1930s, following the Depression and the abandonment of the Gold Standard, he still held a large number of bonds containing 'gold clauses', which declared that the face value and interest were redeemable either in gold coins or a currency equivalent to the value of gold.

In particular he had bought and retained a considerable block of convertible 'gold notes' issued by the British Government in 1917 and redeemable in London or New York. However, gold clauses had by then been declared contrary to the general policy of the United States by a resolution of Congress.

Acting through a trustee on behalf of the bondholders, Plesch brought an action against the British Crown to pay him the face value of these bonds with the accumulated interest in London at a rate equal to the value of fine gold prescribed by the law of the United States in 1917. The Court of Appeal found in his favour in 1936, but the House of Lords later reversed the decision finding that the bonds were governed by the laws of the United States. As a result the Crown was only held liable to redeem the bonds at their face value. Although he made a considerable amount of money, Plesch was furious. He never ceased to believe that he had been tricked. He often used to say that, had it been otherwise, he would have been the richest man in the world.

Arpad Plesch lived in Paris until 1939. During these years he continued his affair with Mrs Ulam. Although he claimed that the affair was a closely guarded secret, it was noted that she travelled about in a Rolls-Royce or Dusenberg. Plesch claimed he moved to France because the Reichstag election gave the Nazis a strong minority and he felt 'that the trend in Germany was toward a political and economic order with which I could not be in sympathy.'[18] He wrote that during this time he was only in transit and he never went back to Germany after 1936. In August 1939, he transferred his domicile to Switzerland.

By this time, under cover of his company, the Maritime, he had purchased the villa at Beaulieu-sur-Mer in the South of France.

During the 1930s Marysia Ulam caused her parents and Plesch more than a few problems, not least because she was irrepressibly promiscuous. In November 1936 it appeared she was about to marry George Randolph Hearst, the eldest son of William Randolph Hearst, but her father disapproved because he was already married and about to get divorced.

Plesch's life changed in 1938, when, on 16 February, Mr Ulam died at the Hotel de Paris in Monte Carlo. Ulam was buried in Monte Carlo, and on 8 July Plesch married his widow in London. At around the same time Marysia found herself in difficulty. She seems to have been married to a man called Krauss as in 1939 she was being described as Madame Ulam-Krauss. At another time Plesch made an arrangement with an Englishman called Cecil Harcourt-Smith, a ruggedly handsome naval commander, that he should marry her. He was a wild character who, some years later – in August 1954 – made a successful double-crossing of the Atlantic with a small crew in his 61ft, twin diesel-engined lifeboat, taking 33 days to sail out but only 23 to return.

The marriage plan did not go well, and Plesch may well have concluded that Harcourt-Smith was well suited to 'double-crossing'. According to Plesch, Harcourt-Smith engaged in 'libels and intrigues', and 'elicited money from me, which was intended to be given to him only after the marriage. Inter alia he gave me an uncovered cheque and committed different other misdeeds*.'[19] Nevertheless Harcourt-Smith did marry Marysia, and two daughters were born to her – Florence or 'Flockie' in June 1939, and a younger Harcourt-Smith daughter, Joanna, in 1946. Later he and Marysia were divorced, he remarried and died in London

---

* Interestingly, when applying for French domcile after the war, Plesch described his son-in-law as an officer in the British Royal Navy, and a British citizen, adding 'the Harcourt Smith family is one of the most honourable in Great Britain.' This was to give an idea of the 'social milieu' to which he belonged.

aged 56, on 18 March 1956.

To move the story of Marysia's children forward a bit, Flockie was the child that Arpad Plesch took under his wing, and later described as his adopted daughter. To her he left a large share of his fortune. She is the mother of Arpad (Arki) Busson, a well-known city trader and generous fundraiser for charity, who lived for some years with the supermodel, Elle Macpherson.

Arpad did not much bother with the younger daughter, Joanna, nor did he bequeath her any money. She reacted against her background. In an interview she described her father, Cecil Harcourt-Smith as a 'secret agent for Britain during the Second World War'[20]. She reacted against her cousin, S.M. Ulam, and the H-Bomb, and became a controversial figure in the 1960s world of counter-culture and the psychedelic movement. She acquired her own celebrity by her involvement with Timothy Leary, the famed advocate of psychedelic drug research.

Leary had been convicted of possession of drugs (a small amount of marijuana) in 1968, and imprisoned. There is no doubt that he was being made an example of by the Nixon administration, because they feared his considerable influence on youth culture, which was huge and therefore dangerous. He escaped to Europe, where Joanna met him in 1972. She underwent a pseudo-occult wedding with him at an hotel.

In 1973 he and Joanna went to Afghanistan, but he was arrested, extradited to the United States and imprisoned in Folsom Prison, California, next to the Sharon Tate murderer, Charles Manson. Joanna was also in Los Angeles and quoted as saying: 'I'm here to free him. Love is what it takes.' Leary was more sanguine: 'I'm going to get a lawyer,' he said.[21]

Today Joanna has her own website, www.metahistory.org , and is engaged in the battle against 'the rush to fulfil the Armageddon scenario by sexually repressed power hungry madmen'. She declares: 'I see love is a conscious choice and a daily practice. I see this nightmare story turning into a tale of ecstasy and gratitude. I see opalescent light and the triumph of tenderness.'[22]

In December 1938 Plesch arrived in New York with Leonie and her pregnant daughter, Marysia, with as yet no grandchildren. He installed his entourage in suites at the Savoy Plaza. With him came a large retinue of servants and a private secretary who could take dictation in five languages. Two Hispano-Suizas also travelled with the party.

Having started life as a citizen of the Austrian-Hungarian Empire, and taken up Hungarian citizenship after the First World War, having paid his first visit to the United States in 1926, and having returned in 1929, 1933, and 1937, the New York visit between December 1938 and June 1939 is significant since his family arrived on Liechtenstein passports. In August 1939 Plesch secured letters of naturalisation from the Republic of Haiti for himself, his wife and her daughter, paying $6,000 for the privilege. One passport that Plesch was never interested in obtaining was a US passport. He declared frequently that he would leave America 'on a Wednesday if by staying until Thursday he might be taxable.'23

Plesch later explained that since 1934 he had acquired a substantial shareholding in the Haitian Corporation of America. On that visit in 1938/39 he undertook the reorganisation of the corporation with the help of the Chase Bank. He visited Haiti. He found that there was a new law allowing 'those with substantial interests in Haiti to acquire Haitian nationality' so he availed himself of this right. He explained: 'I took this step with a great deal of regret, since I had always been a loyal Hungarian subject and considered that I owed much to the old Hungary which gave me birth and education. However, as a non-Aryan I could not ignore the trend in Hungary toward national-socialist ideals, and it was therefore only logical that I should accept the opportunity to acquire the citizenship of a country, however small, in which I had substantial investments.'24

Plesch said he accepted the role of Counsellor of the Haitian Legation in Rome, because, following the invasion of Holland and Belgium, it seemed that Switzerland might be in danger, and

Italy 'seemed to have determined upon a policy of neutrality.' He left Italy two weeks after it entered the war. He retreated to Switzerland. He pointed out that he had never expressed any sympathy for the Axis:

'I am non-Aryan; my fortune is entirely in England or in America; my whole financial position places me in opposition to totalitarian principles. Therefore, leaving entirely aside my personal standpoint, it would be deliberate suicide for me to have or to express any sympathy for the Axis'.[25]

The war presented huge problems for a rich Hungarian Jew. By December 1940 J. Edgar Hoover, Director of the FBI, was writing to his special agent in New York, asking about the 'identities, background and activities' of several individuals, including 'Mr Plesch'.[26] Despite protests from Hoover, nothing was filed until September 1941. Detailed information was then given:

'Arpad Plesch is now living at #2 avenue Victor-Ruffy, Lausanne, Switzerland, with his wife and foster-daughter. In February 1941 they were in Rome, where he has a home at Consigliere, Largo Elvezia 5. He owns a villa at Naples and has an apartment at Blvd Suchet #2, Paris, France, which is now inaccessible to him. Before 1935 he lived in Berlin, Germany, and in Budapest, Hungary, making occasional trips to US'.[27]

In November 1939 Plesch was barred from re-entering French Territory and divided his time between Italy and Switzerland. On 11 January 1940 Great Britain put him, his wife and the daughter on their Blacklist #1, which barred them from all British territory, because 'Plesch is strongly suspected of being an agent for Italy or Germany or both.'[28]

Plesch claimed that the reason that he was on the British Black List was entirely the work of his son-in-law, Cecil Harcourt-Smith. It was 'due to the libel and intrigues of a man named Harcourt S. . . . ' who, on account of having committed his various misdeeds, 'had every interest to keep me away from England, because he was apprehensive of losing his job in case of my prosecuting him for criminal offence.'[29]

The FBI were especially interested in Plesch's American holdings, noting: 'He holds enormous amounts of securities in this country, all well concealed in street names of banks and brokerage houses.'[30]

They noted that in 1922 he and his associates had bankrupted the Haitian-American Corporation and tried to take it over without putting up extra money. Eventually they were forced to invest $200,000 and took it over as the Haitian Corporation of America, a Delaware corporation in 1923. This in turn had six subsidiaries, including a sugar-producing unit with 22,700 acres in Port-au-Prince, a company that first imported rum, then sugar, a railroad company in Haiti (worth $5 million), a company owning the wharf in Port-au-Prince, a financing unit, and a Virgin Island corporation with offices at St Thomas, which used to blend rum.

The FBI were also interested in Plesch's purchase of gold bonds. They believed his pre-war lawsuit in Britain had netted him £10 million. He had tried the same thing in the US, and when he sued the St Louis & Southwestern Railway Co, the judgment had been reversed by the US Supreme Court 'on public policy, in that any other possibility would have bankrupted every railroad in the US.'[31]

By paying $10,000 to a pet charity of the Haitian President, Sténio Vincent, Plesch had got himself appointed Counsellor to the Haitian Legation at Rome, presumably to avoid tax. He had tried to be transferred in this capacity to Washington, but the US State Department had protested. He had tried to buy the Haitian lottery concession in Palm Beach via 'an unknown titled Englishman' (possibly the young Lord Beauchamp) during his visit there in February 1939. The initial conclusion of the FBI agents was damning:*

---

* Even now a number of names in the report have not been released by the FBI.

'Plesch is described as a financial and legal genius without scruples or allegiance, completely self-centred and without any hampering ties of national feelings. [Name withheld] states that Plesch has a terrific lust for power and that if he were to come to the US he would either own it or ruin it in a short time. Little is known of him personally, but he is universally disliked and feared by those who come in contact with him . . .

Subject does not have any record with the New York Police Department. His European record is unknown here. He owns several cars, but they are all in foreign registration. The British government regards him as undesirable and the agent of an enemy alien. He is not known to have engaged in any political activities in this country but his activities are so interwoven with banking and brokerage circles that he wields considerable financial influence'.[32]

It transpired that Plesch was trying to transfer securities from Germany to Haiti via the Swiss American Company in New York. He was hoping to buy one of the finest properties in Port-au-Prince, but the British Minister there reported him as 'a very suspicious character . . . on the British Black List.' A confidential source stated that Plesch was 'known to have Nazi sympathies . . . Plesch has been trying to negotiate the transfer of securities from Switzerland to Haiti . . . The suggestion has been made that these securities may well be German Loot.'[33]

In February 1941 Dr and Mr Plesch were both baptised Roman Catholics in the Vatican, a further transformation. In the same month a 'reliable report' alleged that Plesch was acting as an intermediary in Geneva to distribute Russian gold in France.

In the latter months of 1941 Plesch was soliciting 'various acquaintances in the United States and Canada in his petition for removal of his name from the United States Proclaimed List of Certain Blocked Nationals,'[34] and by January 1942 J. Edgar Hoover was aware of this.

In March 1942 Plesch was in Lausanne, attempting to gain passage on a ship repatriating American diplomats formerly accredited to Axis countries. Constantin Fouchard, Minister for Haiti in Berne, had an interview with him on 28 March. He surprised Plesch by querying his status as Legation Counsellor in Rome, and urged him to clarify this by cabling Port-au-Prince. Fouchard concluded that there was no chance of Plesch travelling to Haiti via the United States:

'Besides just like our notorious "White Niggers" of twelve years ago, the Americans do not seem greatly to value our naturalised Germans who have disguised themselves as Haitians for a quarter of an hour. Though Mr Plesch was not German, but first Hungarian and then Roumanian, if I am not mistaken . . .'[35]

Presently Fouchard reported that Hermann Göring's wife had stayed at Plesch's house on her visit to Lausanne, that Plesch possessed a diplomatic passport with visas for Spain, France, Portugal, and the USA, and with later visas for Argentina and Brazil, that he was being watched by the Swiss police and he urged that Plesch's diplomatic passport be withdrawn.

On 13 August 1942 J. Edgar Hoover alerted Nelson A. Rockefeller, Co-ordinator of Inter-American Affairs, and Adolf A. Berle, Jr, Assistant Secretary of State, about Plesch, his background, and his so-far unsuccessful attempts to induce the Haitian Government to effect his return to Haiti as a Haitian diplomat. It transpired that Plesch lost his Haitian citizenship under a decree of the Haitian Government dated 5 August 1942.

In December 1944 Plesch was still in Switzerland and still on the various black lists. This situation gradually changed in his favour. On 31 May 1945 he was taken off the British Black List, and Lord Selborne, the Minister for Economic Warfare, wrote to him apologising for a very sad injustice occasioned by the vagaries of the war. On 24 July 1946 Selborne further wrote to John Plesch, describing Arpad as the innocent victim of a chain of circumstances, just as there had been many innocent victims of bomb damage.

The war over, many figures found themselves either under arrest or in danger of arrest and trial. In this new atmosphere of intrigue, further allegations were made against Plesch from

Above A marriage of convenience. Count Zsiga Berchtold – husband no. 4.

Above right Gloria Guinness with Charley Buxhoeveden, an early love of Etti's.

Right Dino Philipson – romance blossomed and floundered in 1945.

Below A temporary arrangement. Deering Davis – husband no. 5.

Below right Deering's famous wife, the star of the silent cinema, Louise Brooks.

Above Nicky Nagel – Etti's great love in South America.

Left Security at last. Etti in Rome with Arpad Plesch – husband no. 6.

Below Marital dexterity. Three of Etti's husbands after lunch at the Villa Leonina – Pali Pálffy, Zsiga Berchtold and Arpad Plesch. The lady is Princess Peter of Montenegro (the former music hall dancer, Violet Wegner).

Etti's formidable mother in later life.

Flockie and Bunny before their memorable coming-out ball at Claridge's in May 1956.

Arpad Plesch talking to The Queen after
Bunny's wedding in May 1962.

Bunny and Etti at the Villa Leonina.

A night out at the theatre – Princess Margaret,
Bunny, The Queen and Lord Snowdon.

The happiest day of her life.
Etti in the winner's enclosure with *Psidium*, after the 1961 Derby.

Dr Arpad Plesch.

More racing triumphs. Etti with *Miswaki*, her US/European Stakes winner.

Mrs Bryan Jenks (left) with Bunny and Etti in the winning enclosure at Royal Ascot after Bunny won the Jersey Stakes with her horse, *Tecorno*, June 1983.

Full circle. Etti with her friends, Nancy and Ronald Reagan.

To Etti
With best wishes & love
Nancy & Ron

several quarters. He was accused of being involved in the finances of the Rote Drei network, but 'no shadow of proof of any collaboration of Plesch with a Russian intelligence organisation' was obtained.[36] He was ordered to leave Switzerland but due to an unheard appeal did not have to do so.

In September 1945 Leland Harrison, the US Minister in Bern, alleged that Plesch had been in Milan the previous March, 'working with leading Nazi officials in Italy.' He had been spotted in Gestapo Headquarters at the Hotel Continental. Aldo Neri, who claimed to have worked as a counter-espionage agent for the French, stated that Plesch's friend, Count Ferdinand Thun-Hohenstein, a Wehrmacht officer of Austrian origin, had frequently prepared fake passports for Plesch.[37]

In December 1945 a French National, Jean Walter, instituted criminal proceedings against Plesch for breach of confidence, alleging that he had absconded with funds entrusted to him in June 1940, by transferring all the shares of the French company, La Maritime, to a bank in Berlin. Walter said that the shares were held by Plesch in the name of the Societé Anglo-Continentale, which held title to the Villa Leonie [Leonina] and other real estate in Beaulieu-sur-Mer. Walter claimed that Plesch had sold the building he owned in Berlin to 'an influential member of the Nazi Party' in a transaction conducted in the Hotel Baur au Lac in Zurich.

Walter also reported that when the Germans invaded Paris, they took over 2 Boulevard Suchet as their headquarters, evicting every apartment owner except Plesch, 'a fact the more astonishing in view of Plesch's professed Jewish religion.' In 1941 Plesch was allowed to move his furniture and other assets freely from Paris to Switzerland.

It transpired that Stephan Saner, a Swiss railroad engineer in Lugano, a fervid supporter of the Allies, liked to dabble in the construction of power receiving sets. He was thus able to pick up radio instructions from the Nazis to their agents:

'He further contends that on 11 September 1944, he heard one such station in Germany give instructions that 80,000,000 Swiss francs be deposited for the account of Arpad Plesch and that the Nazi agents contact Plesch to advise him that this money was being deposited for use of Nazi agents in Switzerland and abroad. Saner declares that the messages were transmitted in clear, not in cipher, and that he had never heard of Plesch until these messages came over the station and he then checked to find they were real people. He wrote to Plesch saying that he had received a message about money transactions for him but Plesch replied that he could not discuss it because as a foreigner he could not do business in Switzerland. He is willing to testify to the aforesaid under oath.'[38]

On 26 September 1947 it was reported to the FBI that Plesch, and his secretary, Josef Dembitzer, had set sail from Southampton to New York in the *Queen Elizabeth*. Mrs Plesch was with them. They entered the United States on a visitor visa (being stateless since the Haitians had withdrawn Plesch's passport), and settled in great style at the Savoy-Plaza Hotel, arriving with 20 or 30 trunks, and their own Rolls Royce and chauffeur. The FBI were still watching them and Plesch was interviewed. While he was there, he received a letter from the US State Department, dated 24 November 1947, declaring that he was not an enemy of the United Nations, that he had not given help to the enemy during the war and that he was in the United States with the full approval of the US government.

Brigadier-General Barnwell R. Legge, a somewhat dubious figure,* then wrote Plesch a letter which survived in Etti's papers at the time of her death and confirms what was written:

24 February 1948
Dear Dr Plesch,
I have read with interest the State Department's letter of November 24, 1947, and I am glad to know that they have examined into your case and, although belatedly, fully cleared you of any enemy

* Legge was deemed a traitor to the internees of the Swiss camp, Wauwilermoos, having failed to recognize its existence, as a result of which many were raped, beaten, starved and abused.

adherence or dealings.

As United States Military Attaché in Switzerland during the war I examined into your case on behalf of the War Department and was also familiar with your interviews to the Allied military authorities, and I got to know you well. Your inclusion and retention on the Proclaimed List were outside the military jurisdiction, but your status as a friendly or unfriendly alien was our direct concern. As to the latter, after careful inquiry and investigation, it was abundantly clear to me that you were not unfriendly to the enemy but definitely and decidedly in support of the Allied cause. In fact, you rendered aid of substantial value to the allied military cause with which I am fully familiar and for which both the British Military Attaché and myself have previously expressed our appreciation.

I am familiar with the malicious and false charges made against you during the war. For what purposes these charges were created I do not know, but it was and is clear that you were the unfortunate victim of unwarranted abuse and injustices. Knowing intimately as I do the facts of your background, interests and activities, I am indeed pleased that the injustice and error of your inclusion and retention on the United States Proclaimed List has now, to the extent possible, been rectified.

This letter is written with the permission of the War Department.'39

This was the letter that Arpad Plesch occasionally showed to people.

Meanwhile Plesch spent most of his time ensconced with his attorneys or in meetings at the Chase National Bank. In the same year Plesch won a case against the Banque Nationale de Haiti which had impounded his money, and the Bank was required to release his funds.

At the beginning of 1948 Plesch petitioned the French Government for a transit visa. This was refused. In March James F. Byrnes, Secretary of State in Washington, wrote to confirm that Plesch's name should be lifted from the Black List, and when the columnist, Walter Winchell made a disobliging remark about Plesch in his column of 6 June, Plesch immediately forced a retraction to the effect that he had been 'washed of all suspicion by both the US and British Governments'[40]. In April he was issued with a Special Cuban passport in Havana 'to carry out a special mission for the Cuban government.'[41] He was thus able to enter France, and the Plesch family returned to Switzerland in early summer.

In September 1948 Plesch was having no easier a time with the FBI, Hoover suggesting that 'in view of the vast amount of derogatory information' on Plesch, it was an idea 'to consider the advisability of taking the necessary steps to prevent his re-entry into the United States.'[42]

The Foreign Service in Paris still held him under suspicion as late as March 1951, noting that he was suspected in Switzerland because he travelled a great deal, even during the war, and frequently to Italy; it was believed (though not proved) that he had made financial transactions for the USSR; he had been described as 'a first class agent of Germany' and was supposed to have transferred considerable capital from Germany to Haiti; and finally that he appeared 'to have access to very large sums and to have important interests in a great number of financial, commercial and industrial organisations in various countries.' The Foreign Service noted: 'He is characterised as a cunning, shrewd and suspected man but against whom proof is lacking.'[43]

At about this time he petitioned the French not for a transit visa, or a 'carte de sejour', but for a residents' card. He considered that he had put behind him all the accusations raised against him, none of which had been proved, and he wished with 'a particular passion' to become a resident in a country which he considered his second home, having property at Croissy-sur-Seine and Beaulieu-sure-Mer, speaking French as his second language, and having adopted many of its customs.

Plesch was forced to react against a number of allegations. He pointed out that the allegations made by Jean Walter had come to nothing and that the Swiss authorities had given him a visa to re-enter Switzerland. He stated that a story about microphones being installed in his property at Beaulieu 'to spy on his guests' were nothing more than internal telephones with speakers so that he could issue instructions to his secretaries from one room to another.

He had been accused of having received Japanese agents there, but he pointed out that he had had no contact whatsoever with the Japanese, though he had entertained the Chinese Ambassador, Wellington Koo, and his wife, which was quite different and had given rise to the rumour. He pointed out that he had only been to Germany once since 1933, when travelling from Carlsbad to Salzburg.

They had tried to link him to the Stavisky Affair, a celebrated financial scandal of the mid 1930s, in which many had lost their money to an embezzler. Many people had known Stavisky, including figures such as Mistinguett, but Plesch pointed out that Stavisky had left Paris in December 1933 and died in January 1934.*

He referred to his relations with Koenigswarter, described as a German spy. Plesch admitted knowing him socially, and playing bridge with him. He described him as an Israelite German, who became a Haitian citizen. He had run a fur company and seemed a peaceable man. Plesch declared that he would have been very surprised had he had any contact with the Gestapo.**

Plesch further stated that he had had no dealings with Mme Göring and that it was known that she had never visited Switerland during the war. All these allegations flew about, but nothing was ever proved against Plesch.

On the positive side, Plesch had some good things to say about himself. He noted that his difficulties with the United States

* The Affair was the subject of an Alain Resnais film in 1974, *Stavisky*, starring Jean-Paul Belmondo and Anny Duperey.
** This would appear not to be Baron Jules de Koenigswarter (1904-95), the French resistance hero, who later held diplomatic posts in Norway and Mexico, and who was married to the jazz enthusiast, Nica de Koenigswarter (1913-88), formerly a Rothschild.

ceased, as if by magic, the moment he ceded the majority of his shares in the Haitian Corporation of America. He dismissed the charges of Jean Walter as 'odious' and blamed them entirely for his problems with the Swiss. He pointed out that he had donated large sums to the Red Cross in Lausanne, that he had helped distressed families in France, that in 1943 he had created a foundation for war orphans at his property in Beaulieu, to which had given $50,000, and that on his return to France, he had sold paintings at the Charpentier Gallery (on 26 June 1948) for the benefit of UNAC, raising 1,912,500 French francs.

He had some reasonable points to make. 'It is always difficult to disprove a negative,' he wrote, noting that in civilised countries it is incumbent on the accusers to prove the charge. He thought that the reason people were against him was 'an infantile taste for humanity for the irrational and the mysterious', and on account of his huge fortune. He was 'head of an enormous fortune, perfectly disseminated, of the kind that it is difficult to understand, without being au courant with the details of his affairs and its provenance.'

Then there were the circumstances of his private life (his secret liaison with Mrs Ulam) that had made him appear suspicious. The fact that his property in Germany had been sequestrated and members of his family living in Hungary and Poland interned in concentration camps did not endear the German authorities to him. When in France he had been accused of receiving special favours from these authorities, due to a sign on his door stating 'Property belonging to a consul of the Haitian Legation', but the moment that Haiti had entered the war on the German side, his property had been pilloried by the Germans. As to being a Gestapo agent, he had never professed ideological passions, had his enormous fortune, so was not motivated by money, preferred to be independent and nor did his religion draw him to the Gestapo. He ended his defence by saying: 'When someone harms a dog, the Society for the Protection of Animals takes up the cause of the wretched beast. But there is no society for the protection of stateless persons'.44

On 11 February 1953 the Foreign Service learned that Plesch was in Nice, but planning to travel from France to Jamaica, to visit Haiti and to enter the United States from one of the Caribbean countries. Plesch was now allowed into Britain and went there regularly to see Flockie, travelling with his secretary and valet.

As late as December 1953 came the final conclusion of endless attempts to pin something on Plesch. The FBI informed the American Embassy in Grosvenor Square that Plesch was 'a wealthy scoundrel whose activities have been constantly suspect for one reason or another but who always manages to get away with it.'45 They ceased to investigate him.

Just before the war Plesch had acquired land in Beaulieu-sur-Mer and built the Villa Leonina, which was named after his wife. Leonie died in Paris on 17 January 1951, aged 67, and was buried in a fantastic marble mausoleum in the Catholic Cemetery in Monte Carlo. As she was dying, she asked Arpad to look after Marysia. He agreed to do so, but hoped that she would cease to be as promiscuous as she had previously been. That assurance was given and so, partly to please his late wife, and maybe as a way to keep the jewels in the family, Arpad married Marysia. Susan George thought the marriage was because 'it was too difficult to dispose of Leonina's jewelry. Actually, I saw a couple of the trunks filled with incredible amounts of treasures. Marysia was very strange.'46 He was married to Marysia soon afterwards.

Thus Plesch united the roles of being Flockie's step-grandfather and her stepfather. This was a confusing situation, and one that led to a certain amount of speculation, no doubt ill-founded. Even the FBI were muddled, one report writing of Marysia: 'It is not known whether Plesch is the father of her [Leonie Ulam's] daughter or not.'47 He was not her father.

While married to Marysia, Arpad invited Susan George (his niece by marriage) down to Beaulieu. He did so because he had heard that this Hungarian girl, daughter of a respected friend, the doctor who had looked after the Plesches when young, was living 'the life of an impoverished student and "sale étrangere", as the French called us immigrants.'

During this phase, Arpad asked Susan to help Flockie with her reading and writing. They used to go down to the beach together with paper and pencil, but there were distractions, and she was not entirely successful in her mission. Nor were things going well in the Plesch household. Marysia failed to change her ways. She remained uncontrollably promiscuous and presently Plesch divorced her. She then moved to Paris where she called herself Mrs Plesch. After Etti married Arpad, this caused a certain amount of confusion, particularly in expensive dress-shops where occasionally Marysia's bills were despatched to Liechtenstein and paid in error.

Marysia eventually died of cancer. Arpad continued to care for her daughter, Flockie.

In the early 1950s Plesch had an affair with the neurotic and not very bright Queen Alexandra of Yugoslavia, when she and King Peter were living at Roquebrune, and it was widely known in the South of France that he settled many of her debts, and generally picked up the expenses for a time. That this was condoned by King Peter was not greatly to his credit.

There are conflicting versions of the meeting between Etti and Arpad Plesch. One version has her staying at Claridge's in London and asking the hall porter who was the richest man in the hotel and what were his interests. When she discovered that one of the guests was Dr Plesch and that he liked gardening, she purchased a book on gardens and went up and down in the lift until they ran into each other. Further coincidences were contrived and presently she was sailing round the world with him.

The version of Alexis de Redé, a man who had plenty of time to amass such stories, was that Plesch asked his then confidential secretary, a social man called Duchnitz, if he knew a lady who might be prepared to travel with him. Duchnitz recommended

Etti. After Plesch married her, she took it upon herself to dispense with this secretary's services. 'It was not very nice of her,' recalled the Baron.[48] As we will see, Etti gave contradictory versions of her meeting with Arpad, and we must give her the benefit of the doubt.

Etti almost certainly knew nothing about Arpad Plesch's wartime activities, or of his financial dealings. How much she knew about his marital arrangements is also questionable. It did not particularly interest her.

And what did the Plesch family make of Etti when she appeared in Arpad's life. After her death, some relations who had read her obituary in *The Times*, came to light. Susan George recalled that she remembered 'a lot of the "dirty" details!' as she put it. In particular there was a version that Etti had been a dancer at the Arizona, a well-known rather exciting club in Berlin. This version cannot be true, but it is worth recording as some people believed it and it is therefore indicative of how people thought of Etti:

'In her [Etti's] days, girls did not get too much education, if any at all, in Hungary, who came from the lower classes . . . I am sure that Granny [Mirza] said that she was a chorus girl in the Arizona . . . the most famous nightclub for aristocrats and rich foreigners in Europe . . . Poldi travelled to Budapest only to go there. The only nightclub in the world of that time where naked girls swung from crystal chandeliers, while the patrons ate caviar, foie gras, sipping champagne in sumptuous séparées. I believe, according to Granny , Count Eszterházy fell for her there . . .'[49]

TEN

Husband 6
Dr Arpad Plesch, 1954-1974

Dr Arpad Plesch (1889-1974).
Born Budapest, 25 March 1889.
Married (1) London, 5 July 1938, Leonina
Ulam (1883-1951).
Married (2), ca 1951, Marysia Harcourt-Smith (née Ulam).
Divorced ca. 1953.
Married (3) London, 12 June 1954, Etti Wurmbrand.
Died London, 16 December 1974.

I ARRIVED BACK in Europe where I was immediately invited to stay with Gloria Guinness and her husband Loel in their extraordinary penthouse apartment, high above the Avenue Matignon. I had known Gloria since her early days in Berlin, when she was a friend of Freddy Horstmann's and when she was married to Franz-Egon von Fürstenberg. At the end of the war that marriage was dissolved. Although the frontiers were almost completely closed, Gloria managed to leave Germany and, taking a few jewels with her, settled in Madrid. She stayed in the Ritz, where she had a tiny room. People said later she might have been a spy, but I don't believe that.

Gloria could have been a figure from Lesley Blanch's wonderful book, *The Wilder Shores of Love*. Recently she has been consigned to the kind of 'style' articles that appear in certain magazines. She was worth so much more, taking great risks in her life.

I visited her there and she told me she hardly had any money left, but true to a life-long rule to stay on top as long as she could, she was spending what remained of her funds at the best hotel in Madrid. It was a kind of investment, I suppose. Everyone knew she was staying at the Ritz. She told me: 'Once you go down, it is very difficult to rise again! I intend to remain on top as long as I possibly can!'

I remember we sat in the hall of the Ritz and I looked at her. She was as beautiful as ever, still well dressed and the centre of considerable attention. Many Spaniards, grandees, diplomats and generals joined us at her table. I believe that it was while staying at the Ritz that she first met her future husband, Loel Guinness, a famously rich financier.

Since then I have always advised girls that if they want to marry a rich man, they must go to the best hotel in the city. That is where these men can be found, and also in casinos, which Gloria loved and where she spent a lot of her time.

Before Loel, Gloria was married to a small Egyptian called Prince Ahmed Fakhry, not very elegant, and they lived at one time at the Crillon in Paris. Like Louise de Vilmorin and at about the same time, I have to say, she was one of the mistresses of Duff Cooper.

After her divorce from Fakhry, there was a time when two men were desperate to marry her. One was Lord Beatty and the other was Loel. Gloria could not make up her mind, but eventually she settled for Loel, and they were married in April 1951.

Now that Gloria was married to one of the richest men in Europe, she seemed more beautiful than ever. Soon she had houses in Florida, Mexico, and Normandy, near Guy de Rothschild's house. She was fun, elegant and full of life. Her greatest achievement as far as houses were concerned was a lovely house in Acapulco, all open, with no windows. In some ways though, Gloria and Loel were not well matched. He made her live a life that she did not really like.

As I said, she liked casinos, and staying up late at night. Loel was the opposite. He liked his dinner at 8.30 every night. So when she married Loel, there were no casinos, no gambling and no late nights. She had everything she wanted, plenty of money to spend, but I think she missed the fun. She had a very beautiful daughter, Dolores. In 1955, Dolores married Loel's son by Joan Yarde-Buller, Patrick, and they had a son and two daughters, but he was killed in a motor accident in 1965. Then Dolores fell madly in love with Karim Aga Khan, the son of Joan by her marriage to Aly Khan, and wanted to marry him, but nothing came of that eventually.

A few days after my arrival in Paris Loel and Gloria gave a dinner party for me. There were many guests from French and English society, and many diplomats, but there was another more mysterious man, Arpad Plesch.

He was not tall, in fact only just taller than me, but I thought him very good looking with most intelligent dark eyes, which moved about as he spoke, taking in and understanding every situation at once. He seemed to look deep into peoples' souls. Gloria had not put him next to me at dinner for reasons of protocol, and there was another man and another woman between us, so that I could only catch a few bits of what he said. Though I understood Gloria's adherence to the rules of the table, I was inwardly quite furious, and so after dinner, in the drawing room, I made him pull up a chair at my side, which he did instantly.

I discovered that he spoke French, English, or German with a slight Hungarian accent which I particularly liked. So we spoke of Hungary. He told me of his family, his life in Vezprém, his famous brother, the doctor, but try as I could, I was unable to get him to reveal much about himself. Loel filled me in later, telling me he was a financial genius who had made a huge fortune before the war. I remembered that the Henschels had told me how, as early as 1933, when Hitler came to power, they had been offered the chance to buy two beautiful Plesch houses in Berlin and just outside it, but that the purchase could not take place because the Nazis confiscated all he had in Germany.

By this time Arpad's interests were not in Germany fortunately, but abroad. Arpad normally foresaw most things and he had foreseen the tragic end of our dear country, Hungary. He had moved to Switzerland, with interests in Haiti. He acquired a large stretch of land in Haiti, where sugar was planted, and being lucky, this soon turned out to be the most valuable land in Haiti. He invested substantially in his country of adoption and the returns were enormous. Now, after the war, he pursued his business interests from his homes, his villa in Beaulieu, his apartment in the Avenue Foch in Paris, or from wherever he happened to be travelling at the time.

Loel told me that Arpad pursued any kind of business that was honest. He said he liked 'the so-called special situations. Through a world-wide network of friends and consultants, he usually learns earlier than other people or banks when a firm is in trouble, and in need of credit; or when a new stock issue is being prepared; or when it is a good moment to start a law suit against a government, when other people were afraid to do so.' He had also made some wise investments, not least in the lucrative Societé des Bains de Mer in Monte Carlo.

Loel told me the story of how Arpad had sued the British Government over the gold clause. The big banks all advised him not to proceed, warning him that he would incur huge costs, but Arpad was a shrewd lawyer and bought up a lot of undervalued stock. The case was an international sensation.

I came away most impressed by Arpad. Loel painted quite a picture of him, and others backed up what he said. From that first meeting I was fascinated by him.

As it happened, I was in London soon after this, and whether or not consciously remembering Gloria's advice about hotels, I was at Claridge's. So too was Arpad who, at that time, was putting Flockie into school at Hatherop Castle. Though Bunny was still in Chile, I mentioned that I might put her there too. He said he was going back to Paris on a certain flight, and soon I too was on the same flight. He told me that shortly he was setting off on a voyage to Japan to collect specimens for his botanical garden, and at the same time to consider investing in Tokyo.

We saw a lot of each other in the coming weeks. He took me racing at Longchamp and Auteuil, gave luncheon and dinner parties for me at his gorgeous flat, took me to Maxim's and other great restaurants. His conversation was always fascinating, and I soon realised – he was the man of my life!

He was twenty-five years older than me. Cecilia Sternberg wrote that she thought I was looking for a father figure. Arpad was a kind and wise man and the way he took care of me could be deemed to have a slightly paternal streak. I was attracted by his intelligence, his youthful spirit and his generosity.

Much earlier in his life, Arpad had been widowed once and then divorced once. Not long before I met him he had had an affair with Queen Alexandra of Yugoslavia. People spoke of his friendship with the King and Queen of Yugoslavia as being like a *ménage à trois*. They were living at Roquebrune not far from his villa and the three of them were frequently together. Arpad paid off a number of Queen Alexandra's debts.

When Arpad set off round the world in search of rare botanical plants, I went with him on the long cruise. When we returned, we stayed at the Grand Hotel in Rome. I sent for Bunny, who arrived from Chile with but one suitcase containing both her summer and her winter clothes. She met Arpad for the first time. A new life began for all of us.

Bunny has often told me since that she was rather surprised by how badly dressed Arpad was. One of the first things I did on our return was to cast a woman's eye over Arpad's wardrobe. Arpad may have been a wizard financier, but he was by no means a sharp dresser. I was not impressed by Arpad's suits, so I whisked him off to Anderson and Sheppard and he soon emerged a well dressed man.

Not long after that, quite timidly, he asked me to marry him. I was surprised to find such shyness in such a great man. As I got to know him, I discovered that there was an inherent shyness in him. I found that attractive.

Soon we were married. In fact I married my sixth husband twice. First I married him in London on 12 June 1954 and then I married him again in Rome on 11 January 1958. Thus began a very happy phase of my life.

I was now well cared for and could look after Bunny and my mother, who also returned to Europe and settled in the South of France. One thing still worried me. Bunny's father, Tommy Esterházy, was living in poor straits in Geneva, although I must say he still managed to remain an elegant man even on a tight budget, always well dressed and with well polished shoes. But I asked Arpad if he would help him. It is a testament to his all encompassing generosity that he gave Tommy an allowance for the rest of his life.

On the other hand we had to live in an atmosphere of some prejudice. Anyone who is as successful as Arpad is bound to be hedged about by rumours, often unfairly. There is still a sealed file in the Public Record Office indicating that his name was on a black list in Washington in 1949 for alleged wartime activities. He showed the list to Bunny once. While we were married, Arpad received an official letter of apology for this from the US State Department, but it does not prevent the mud from sticking. The English are of course extraordinarily suspicious of money, especially if they don't know where it comes from. It was something we had to live with.

LIFE WITH ARPAD

Following our marriage, Arpad and I made our home in Paris in his apartment on the Avenue Foch, and at the Villa Leonina at Beaulieu-sur-Mer in the South of France. Suddenly we were all living in great style with eighteen servants at the villa, and more in Paris. We had cars and chauffeurs and it was a happy contrast to live in comfort after many difficult years. I am afraid to say that it was not difficult to take to that way of life and to think of it as normal.

I never had an allowance of my own. When I wanted something, I just bought it or ordered it, so if I went to Balenciaga, they sent the bill to Liechtenstein and it was paid. Many may find that a curious way to run things, but that is how it was. Sometimes things went wrong, as Marysia was still in Paris and still used the name of Madame Plesch. Sometimes her bills landed in Arpad's office too, which was very tiresome.

Arpad had bought the Villa Leonina before the war, naming it after his first wife, the former Mrs Ulam, Marysia's mother. He could have bought any of the finest villas in that part of the Côte d'Azur, and he certainly looked at two of the loveliest villas, the Leopolda and La Fiorentina. Unfortunately he chose the Leonina because it was a bargain. The Leonina was a large, comfortable yellow villa. Outside the main gates stood two handsome stone lions, which I gave to Prince Rainier when I gave the villa up after Arpad's death.

The trouble with the Leonina was that it was set in a curious and not very satisfactory location, just behind the port at Beaulieu, close to the road. Though the garden was large, it backed against the well-known railway line that runs from Spain to Italy and is such a feature of the South of France and which has disrupted the tranquillity of so many of the Côte d'Azur's famous villas. With the traffic dividing the villa from the sea at the front, and the train at the back literally silencing any telephone call if a train happened to go past, it was an enclosed place. I suppose the trouble with going for a bargain is that there is always a reason why it is not in great demand.

A better feature of the villa was its celebrated botanical garden, which Arpad had planted himself, becoming a respected expert in the field. The botanical garden stretched high on the hills above the villa and there was a charming guest house in the park, opening towards the sea. Arpad loved this garden and was an expert on the exceptional collection of rare plants and trees it contained. During the war, the garden had been sadly neglected while he had retreated from the South of France to Switzerland, but he had already worked hard to reverse the neglect. He employed twenty gardeners and a botanist.

Arpad loved to have experts come and see the garden and the whole enterprise gained considerable renown in the international horticultural world. I too became interested in the garden but I made it clear from the start that I would not be putting on gardening gloves or doing any deadheading. I was more interested in my horses.

The villa was exquisitely furnished and there were paintings by Picasso, Modigliani and Dufy as well as his enormous library, filled with books on history, sociology and above all botany, of which Arpad had amassed an important collection. I was surprised not only by the quantity and quality of his books, but that he seemed to know what was inside them all! He read quickly and he remembered what he read. He had an extraordinary memory, and did everything he could to keep it in good order. He never ate butter, saying it created cholesterol, while he devoured tropical fruits grown in his own botanical garden. These I found too sour. Frequently he urged our guests to try them. I watched their faces as they pretended to enjoy them.

Arpad's library also included a rare and important collection of pornographic volumes. In his old age Sir Winston Churchill used to spend part of the winter staying in the South of France either with Lord Beaverbrook or his French publisher, Emery Reves – to the occasional annoyance of Lady Churchill, stirred up by snide remarks from Daisy Fellowes. (Wendy Reves was said to be rather too keen on Winston!).

Arpad invited Sir Winston to the Leonina to see the botanical volumes. He duly arrived but soon made his preferences clear. As Arpad produced some volumes on plants, Sir Winston brushed them aside. 'Forget about those,' he said. 'I want to see the pornographic ones.' My husband gave him a thorough viewing of these fine and unusual volumes. I can still see him sitting contentedly in the hall, engrossed in the books, cigar smoke circling about him.

Arpad hated working in an office, so he worked at home. Of course he had an office for his papers and bookkeeping and general files. This work was undertaken by Monsieur Marx, his long-term secretary. He knew every penny that Arpad owned, though he never told me about that side of Arpad's life. Every morning Arpad stayed in bed, telephoning his agents and advisers all over the world, in Tokyo, New York, Buenos Aires, and of course Zurich. He took advice for his future dispositions and he gave advice too. His business friends were keen to stay in touch with him. One of them, the President of one of the big Swiss banks, even tracked Arpad down to the Baur au Lac in Zurich on a Sunday and suggested sending his car for him to 'show him the beauties of the landscape around Zurich!' For a Swiss banker to give up his Sunday in this way proves it had to be worth his while!

Arpad and I travelled a great deal, often with the Guinnesses on their yacht, while on other occasions we went to San Francisco, Honolulu, and other places. Most of them I liked but I did not care for Tokyo, which Arpad took me to as he was making big investments in Japan. We went often to England, not to invest, but to enjoy ourselves. I have always loved England, largely because it is a monarchical country, and when there is a monarchy, there is always a high standard of behaviour and good manners. In England you could find a true gentleman, something which was becoming scarcer and scarcer in European countries. Arpad and I also liked the way they treated their animals. They were much kinder to them than in other countries. But we could not live in England, because of the exorbitant taxes imposed on rich foreigners. So we could but visit.

The Leonina was the setting for many parties, even in the years before I became its chatelaine. After one such party in August 1952, a year or so before I met Arpad, there occurred a terrible accident. Arpad's guests included Gianni Agnelli, then at the height of his five-year love affair with Pamela Churchill (later Mrs Harriman). Pam was meant to be in London. At this party, Gianni met a beautiful brunette girl called Anne-Marie d'Estainville. They had a flirt together and he invited her back to see the Leopolda, the lovely villa above Cap Ferrat, which he then owned.

Gianni and the girl were in an embrace on the terrace at 3 a.m., when to his horror Pam arrived home unexpectedly. She was furious, threw something at them and tried to hit them both. Gianni then drove Anne-Marie back to the Leonina.

Pretending to have said good night to her, he met her in his Fiat station wagon and drove her in the direction of her home on Cap Martin. By then it was after 4 a.m. Gianni drove very fast. He had probably had too much to drink. Anne-Marie became concerned and not without good reason. He missed the entrance to the Cap Roux tunnel and drove right into a butcher's truck with three passengers inside. They were pinned against the mountainside, all of them badly injured. Anne-Marie was spirited away from the scene by friends, while Gianni suffered a broken jaw and badly fractured leg. He ended the night in a hospital in Cannes, where Pam joined him.

Gianni very nearly lost his leg on account of gangrene. Pam nursed him, but his family closed round him and presently that affair was over. Pam moved on to new and greater pastures.

BUNNY'S PARTY

During the season we came to London. Arpad's dark green Rolls Royce with great lanterns on either side was soon a regular feature, parked outside the front door of Claridge's in London. I think people were intrigued by us, especially when we began to entertain.

Presently Bunny left school and it was time to launch her into society. Arpad was also ready to launch his granddaughter, Flockie, so we gave the two girls a joint party at Claridge's in May

1956. By this time, Bunny was well known in Europe. She spoke English, French, Italian, German and Spanish. After Hatherop Castle, she went to Cygnet House, a finishing school in Queen's Gate. In March 1956 she was one of several hundred debutantes presented at court, in her case by the Belgian Ambassadress, the Marquise du Parc Locmaria.

We duly took two suites at Claridge's for the season, a period of about four months. We decided to give a ball for 700 with a seated dinner at the hotel. You have no idea what a fuss this caused in the British press.

We took over the whole of the ground floor of Claridge's and asked Felix Harbord to design the ball in 18th century style. He built raised platforms of artificial stone to create a veranda with box hedges of topiary. He constructed painted pavilions of celadon green and turquoise blue, so that the older guests could sit out and watch the dancing. An illusion of moonlight was created by special effect. One of the rooms was set aside for candlelit suppers and another became a banana grove. The sculptor, Eric Rutherford, made fourteen plaster figures, each about two feet high, to support the trellis work. The effect was magical and there is no doubt that it was 'the most spectacular ball of the season'. Not being overly impressed by the cooking at Claridge's in those days, we brought our own chef from Paris to produce the dinner.

As we were relative newcomers to the London scene we asked Judy Montagu to advise us whom to invite. She was well connected and greatly enlivened the guest list with people like the Duke and Duchess of Argyll, Lord Carnarvon, the Blandfords, Lord Wilton, Lord Dudley and Billy Wallace.

The press decided the party was going to cost £5,000 and remarked that this was £2,000 more than the recent evening party there given by Bulganin and Krushchev. I was forever being caught on the telephone. I told one journalist: 'It is such an uninteresting little party. There must be parties like this every night in London. The cost? I haven't the faintest idea – a few thousands, yes, but really it will be nothing extravagant.' As for the dinner, we began with caviar for the fifty-six guests. We ended the evening with champagne buckets filled with milk, as Arpad believed that milk was good for young people.

In the midst of this press activity, there was the story that the party was to be vetoed by members of the House of Lords. Apparently a memo had been sent around the House of Lords and House of Commons advising members not to attend the party on account of Arpad's so-called wartime activities. I need hardly say that all those invited from the Palace of Westminster duly turned up and had a very good evening.

The party itself was wonderful, and went on until six a.m. Hardly was it over than there was more fuss in the British press. The *New Statesman and Nation* ran an article called 'Bunny, Flockie and Co.' informing their readers that the splendours of our party had been 'duly communicated to the British workers, in goggling detail, by the daily press.' Their leader writer hit out in every direction, describing the party as an example of 'the fake economic prosperity of Tory rule' breeding 'a fake revival of the leisured class.' He went on:

'Ultimately, then, the upper-class spending spree – of which the 1956 Season is the apotheosis – is a form of collective hallucination, a desperate attempt, on the part of Britain's financial and social elite, to persuade itself that nothing has changed. Every all-night party, every case of champagne, every hamper of *pâté de foie gras* is one more proof that the Welfare State no longer exists – has, indeed, never existed – that the Labour government was just a transitory nightmare, that equality is not merely not just around the corner, but receding into the remote distance.'

He ended this diatribe by asking: 'If, as we are constantly told, Britain can never regain her industrial supremacy until the workers identify themselves more explicitly with the nation as a whole, do Bunny, Flockie and Co. really help matters? Nobody would go so far as to suggest that the battle of the export trade is being lost on the dance-floor of Claridge's, but is it too much to ask, just once, that the people at the top should set something other than the worst possible example?'

Other journalists responded by attacking the anonymous writer. One of them was Flockie's uncle, Simon Harcourt-Smith, a somewhat retrograde author and journalist, whose career fell apart when a reviewer pointed out that his biography of Isabelle d'Este was an all too literal translation from someone else's book in Italian. He pointed out that the party was not paid for from 'the pockets of British workers,' but might 'be regarded as an importation of foreign capital which may well have benefited some British workers in the London luxury trades.' The controversy raged on in the *Spectator* and elsewhere.

Bunny enjoyed her season, though she had one awkward moment. The highlight of that year was the ball that the Duke and Duchess of Norfolk gave in London, attended by the Queen. The guests not only wore white tie but also decorations, the Duke and the Queen both wearing the blue riband of the Order of the Garter. Bunny was invited to this party, but unfortunately Flockie was not. So Bunny had to creep out quietly without Arpad knowing, since he would have been hurt by the omission of his ward. Such are the occasional tedious problems of society life.

BUNNY'S MARRIAGE

Bunny's name was soon linked with many famous bachelors, sometimes rightly, sometime wrongly. Her English was soon better than her German, French or Spanish. Not long afterwards, Bunny and Flockie spent a year travelling around the United States, taking in New York, the mid-West, Mexico, Venezuela and other South American countries.

One day, in March 1962, Bunny announced that she had fallen in love with a young Scotsman, Dominic Elliot, second son of the Earl of Minto, an eccentric Scottish peer, and his good looking

Canadian wife, one of four Cook sisters from Montreal, two of whom married Scottish peers*and ended up living near each other in the Borders. Domi was a friend of the Royal Family, in particular Princess Margaret, and often took Bunny out to Windsor Castle. He was then working in an advertising firm.

They became engaged and we held the wedding at St Mary's, Cadogan Street, on 4 May 1962. Tommy, her father, came to London from Geneva to give her away and we decorated the whole church in the Esterházy colours, blue and yellow. It was not long before Tommy died and he was already pale with illness.

Because Domi was such a friend of the Royal Family, many of them came to the reception at 18 Carlton House Terrace, the home of Lord Astor of Hever, overlooking St James's Park. The Queen came, and so did Princess Margaret and Lord Snowdon and the Duke and Duchess of Gloucester. We had 400 guests and filled the house with Arum lilies. We had won the Derby the year before and I remember Arpad talking to the Queen about racing and explaining his theory of the Parabolic Index.

We had a West Indian calypso band outside to which many of the guests danced in the road, and there was a white sugar rabbit on top of the three-tier wedding cake. As it was a Friday, several of the guests brought their children with them before going away for the weekend. We decided to give some of the guests a white Angora rabbit as a present. There were thirty-one of these in cardboard boxes in the hall on the way out. Of course the children all wanted one, but we were not always popular with their parents. Nor were we popular with the RSPCA when a rumour spread that left-over rabbits were destined for the stew.

Bunny and Dominic had two sons, Alexander and Esmond, but were divorced in 1970. I have often hoped that Bunny would re-marry, but she is happiest on her own, based in Monte Carlo, and travelling to remote parts of the world.

---

* Another sister married the Earl of Haddington.

ELEVEN

The South of France

OUR MAIN HOME was in the South of France. The French Riviera has now been my home for nearly fifty years and I must be one of the few people who can remember Monte Carlo in the years before 1920.

I knew the Côte d'Azur in the days when there was no summer season, when people came there to avoid the winter climate, leaving as soon as the sun cast its first rays of heat. King Leopold II of the Belgians settled on Cap Ferrat, building himself a villa which he called Les Cèdres at Saint-Jean-Cap-Ferrat. In 1896 Queen Victoria took over the Grand Hotel at Cimiez, high above Nice, but became annoyed that another building obscured the fabulous view. The following spring she went to the Excelsior Hotel Regina. Most afternoons she went for drives along the coast in her own carriage with her impressive outriders, naturally causing the local inhabitants to stare at her in some amazement. Numerous other celebrated characters, both good and bad, came to Monte Carlo to gamble.

There are two famous descriptions of Monte Carlo. Colette described it as 'a principality whose only boundaries are flowers', while Somerset Maugham, the brilliant but embittered old novelist, who lived at Cap Ferrat, called it 'a sunny place for shady people.'

The winter season gave way to a summer season in the mid 1920s, almost by accident. Cole Porter asked the proprietor of the Hotel du Cap to keep a few rooms open for the summer season, and an American couple, Gerald and Sara Murphy, who settled near La Garoupe invited writers such as Ernest Hemingway and Scott Fitzgerald, who drew on their lives for his novel, *Tender is the Night*. Before the war, the Hotel du Cap had built Eden Roc, with a swimming pool hewn out of the rock. It was not so unusual to see Marlene Dietrich, George Raft, Norma Shearer, Charles Boyer and others soaking up the sun.

PRINCE RAINIER AND PRINCESS GRACE

We had fabulous neighbours at Beaulieu, who greatly enriched the variety of our lives. First and foremost were Prince Rainier and Princess Grace. The Prince loved animals. Arpad had known him in his bachelor years. He used to come over and ask his advice about financial matters, Arpad being a major shareholder in the Societé des Bains de Mer.

It may be that Arpad effected a curious change to the future of Monte Carlo because in 1953 he sold his shares in the Bains de Mer to Aristotle Onassis, the Greek ship-owner who was such a feature of life in the South of France during those years,. Thus Onassis gradually acquired a controlling interest in the company. Onassis saw the development possibilities of Monte Carlo and from that early purchase came the Sea Club, the harbour swimming pool, the new Sporting Club and much more besides. To begin with Prince Rainier kept saying: 'What a nice man Mr Onassis is! He is great fun.' Later that all changed, and the Prince had the famous quarrel with him, eventually issuing more shares and buying him out – somewhat below value as Onassis always said. Onassis last visited Monte Carlo in 1966.

It was an exciting day when the Prince announced his engagement to the beautiful Grace Kelly from Philadelphia. We were invited to the wedding in the Cathedral in the old town of Monte Carlo on the rock where the Palace stands. The combination of Mediterranean prince and Hollywood star caught the attention of the world's press who descended on Monte Carlo in droves.

Besides the usual reporters, there were a number of rather grander celebrities covering the event. Naturally columnists such as Elsa Maxwell and Louella Parsons had plenty to say, but so too did Loelia, Duchess of Westminster, commissioned to write a series of articles for *The News of the World*. Loelia thought the press behaved like savages, and recalled that there were cameramen behind every column and lenses poking through the flowers. One photographer even climbed onto the altar and held onto the cross. Loelia had not been asked to the reception, but Lady Diana Cooper and my erstwhile sparring partner, Louise de Vilmorin, smuggled her in.

The wedding was attended by many of our friends, Enid, Lady Kenamre in pale blue satin, Daisy Fellowes in mauve, Gloria Guinness in pale green and a turban trimmed with gardenias.

I agreed with Loelia Westminster that the American ladies did not excel in their choice of hats, however. She described these amusingly:

> 'One particularly startling hat was a shuttlecock of turquoise blue aigrettes moored – by suction I presume – to the middle of her head. Another was a jewel-studded Tibet cap lavishly decorated on either side with large pink roses. Then there was an enormous shocking pink felt tray that must have obscured the view of many unfortunate enough to be behind it!'

Aristotle Onassis was much in evidence during the week of the wedding, entertaining lavishly aboard his yacht, *Christina*. Loelia was one of the guests for a lunch at which a red-coated band of American collegians played jazz, and Ari seized one of their straw boaters and wore it all afternoon. Graham and Kathy Sutherland, Dame Margot Fonteyn and her husband, Roberto Arias, were amongst the guests.

For me, there was one evening which should have been spectacular, but ended in disaster. I ordered a heavily embroidered gown of white satin for the gala at the Sporting Club. At the dinner a clumsy waiter dropped a hot lobster into my lap. Was there a touch of irony in the way that Loelia wrote of this accident? 'Perhaps the saddest memory I have is the unhappy accident that befell poor Madame Arpad Plesch . . . '

Prince Rainier and Princess Grace frequently came over from the Rocher or their summer residence, Rocagel, high above Monte Carlo. Princess Grace used to say that Arpad was a man from whom you always learned something new. It's true. He was interested in so many different things and always put an unusual slant on things. People loved talking to him. And we loved talking to them.

I was devoted to Rainier and Grace, and found them charming guests. I often said to myself that even if they had not had the position they had, I would always have been very fond of them. Grace did much for Monte Carlo. In 1968 she founded the Garden Club, the idea of which was to improve knowledge of flowers and gardening as well as to stage charity events. At Christmas the members took on the responsibility of decorating the homes of the old people of Monaco. Grace then established an annual *Concours de Bouquets* in May and asked Arpad and me for advice about international judges. We talked to Charles de Noailles and Julia Clements and George Smith were chosen. I was one of the unserious judges along with Monsieur Alexandre, the famous hairdresser, Marc Bohan of Dior, and the novelist, Anthony Burgess, who had settled in Monte Carlo. As a result of this, Grace became a recognised expert on flower arranging and an international judge of such competitions. All this was very much following Colette's lovely description of Monaco.

As I said before, after I left the villa, I gave Prince Rainier the two lions that guarded the villa's gates. He has these at his home in the mountains, and the villa's new owners have now replaced the lions with lions of their own.

I will never forget the shock we all felt when we heard that Grace had had an accident and how we waited as she lay in the hospital and the terrible sadness when we heard that they had switched off the life support machine. As is inevitable when a well-loved figure dies young, there is always distressing speculation. There was nothing unusual about the way she died. All her family was prone to strokes. Her mother suffered one and her brother died from one without any prior warning, again at a young age. Grace was not well and it could have happened at any time. It was made the more horrible by happening when she was driving, which she rarely did, and with her daughter, Stephanie, sitting beside her.

Sometimes, when an old king dies, there is a new lease of life as the heir takes over. But Grace could not be replaced. With her death a light went out of Monte Carlo that can never be rekindled. There are still queues of people walking past her modest grave in the cathedral with its Latin inscription, but when I walk past the souvenir shops, I am surprised that where there used to be a huge selection of postcards of her, now there are none. But she is not forgotten.

I am proud to be on the board of the Princess Grace Foundation. This was founded by Princess Grace in 1964 in order to reach out to those with special needs and for whom the social services did not provide. It works for children in need and provides preventative medicine and treatment for children. It also focuses directly in education and training for young performing artists in Europe and America. It has three major outlets – the Princess Grace Academy of Classical Dance, to train young dancers and continue their general education; the Princess Grace Irish Library (in which I take a particular interest) – this is a wonderful memorial to the Princess and has had an important literary influence in the world: and the Boutiques du Rocher, where local craftsmen and women can sell traditional handiwork. Since Princess Grace's death, Princess Caroline has stressed the importance of the philanthropic work of the Foundation.

Amongst their activities they modernize hospitals in France and the third world, award a generous prize to an artist under the age of 40, give grants to young dancers and pupils, and support the *Première Rampe*, a festival of circus acts by children. My friend,

Virginia Gallico, has always been much involved with the administration and takes care of the Princess Grace Irish Library.

Each year we have meetings in America, which are great fun. We once went to Hollywood and visited the film sets, and we fund-raise to make the necessary money to support all the projects.

LORD BEAVERBROOK

Max Beaverbrook, the celebrated Canadian newspaper magnate and owner of the *Daily Express* was another neighbour. He lived at a Barry Dierks villa, La Capponcina, on Cap d'Ail, which he had bought in 1939, just before the outbreak of the war. Arpad became a friend of his after the war, through a shared interest in pictures and books. Arpad was always buying books at Quaritch in London, from whom he amassed a fine collection.

Lord Beaverbrook was a somewhat mercurial benefactor. He wanted to make the University of New Brunswick the foremost political library in the world and succeeded in buying the papers of certain British politicians for the library, including those of Lloyd George. He also donated books to the library. Any literary figure who reviewed a book for a Beaverbrook paper had to send it back, and very often it made its way to the library. Max sent them all sorts of books, not all of which were the kind of book normally found in a university library, for example the memoirs of Tallulah Bankhead, inscribed to Max.

In 1956 he founded the Beaverbrook Art Gallery at Fredericton, also in New Brunswick, and bought pictures for them. He enriched this collection with important modern British pictures by Sickert, Graham Sutherland, Lucian Freud, Sir John Lavery and Wyndham Lewis.

Arpad was a great supporter of both these projects and generously gave him a great number of special books and pictures for these collections. However, Max never showed any interest in seeing the pornographic volumes.

It was through Max that we met Sir Winston Churchill, who often stayed with him.

Lord Beaverbrook had moments of generosity. He admired the portrait painter, Graham Sutherland, and when his wife Kathy mentioned a desirable house she had fallen for at Menton he gave her £5,000 so that they could buy it.

GRAHAM SUTHERLAND

Graham Sutherland was a marvellous painter. These days, he is of course remembered for the controversial portrait of Sir Winston Churchill that he painted to mark his eightieth birthday and which was presented to him in Westminster Hall in November 1954. The painting greatly upset Sir Winston, and even more so, Lady Churchill. It was taken back to Chartwell, their Kent home, and never seen again. Only after Lady Churchill's death, did their daughter, Mary Soames, reveal that her mother had destroyed it.

Graham Sutherland painted celebrated portraits of a number of our famous neighbours. Somerset Maugham sat for him, as did Max Beaverbrook in 1950 and 1951. Max liked his portrait, even if the art historian, Quentin Bell, described it as 'very much like a diseased toad in methylated spirits.'

Prince Max-Egon von Fürstenberg was painted between 1958 and March 1959. The story of his portrait had a sad end. Graham and Kathy went to deliver it to Donaueschingen Castle in April that year and the Prince joked about a guttering candle portrayed near his left hand. 'Does it mean I have just one year to live?' He smiled. They all dined together and went to their rooms. But Max-Egon died in the night. Of course the Sutherlands thought that somehow the portrait had killed him, but were reassured by the family that Max-Egon had been very unwell and that the portrait had given him great joy at the very end of his life.

We met the Sutherlands through Douglas Cooper, the famous art dealer and collector, who was a friend and neighbour in the South of France. At that time he was a great promoter of Graham's and admired him enormously. In 1956 Arpad asked Graham to paint his portrait. Sittings did not begin until 1959, some undertaken at the Leonina and others at Claridge's. Graham was more used to painting either just heads or full-length portraits. With Arpad he attempted something different, a head with the lower part of the portrait just showing his arms, one of which rests on a pair of library steps. In his right hand Arpad holds a red book, to symbolize his passion for collecting. (Apparently this was a device often used in European portraiture – for example, Moroni's portrait of Giovanni Antonio Pantera in the Uffizi in Florence).

As work progressed in March 1960, Graham told Douglas that he thought he had finished the portrait but decided that the lower part was awful. He had, as he put it, 'mucked it up in trying to get the lower part of the image at rest.' So he had to work hard to recapture his original plan.

The work took shape at Graham's studio in Menton in May 1961 and at the end of that September, the artist brought the finished portrait over to the Leonina for our approval. Graham's biographer described the portrait as follows: 'He had shown the shrewd old man, head and shoulders, against a fawn background, staring outwards, full-face, with hard-boiled eyes; strangely accentuated fingers clasped a symbolic book, presumably botanical.' Actually the background was an abstract interpretation of a curtain.

We were all a bit silent. Arpad made polite noises about it being a work of genius, but said he would have preferred a brighter background. Bunny liked it as it was. Graham decided not to tamper with it, and instead he painted another version, this time with a red background. When it was finished, Graham brought it to London and showed us both the portraits at a dinner at Max Beaverbrook's flat. Arpad bought the red version, paying Graham

£1,500 for it, instead of the original fee, £3,500.

The story did not end there. I gave Flockie the red version after Arpad died, and Graham generously gave me the fawn version, which I still have. In June 1977 I loaned this portrait – a study for the definitive portrait, it is called – to the major retrospective exhibition of Graham's work put on by the National Portrait Gallery to mark the Silver Jubilee of the Queen. There were also quite a few preliminary sketches shown, to give an idea of the development of these portraits. Unfortunately the critics were a bit negative about the pictures, William Packer of the *Financial Times* being particularly critical of the depiction of Arpad's hands.

We liked the Sutherlands but sadly they fell out with Douglas Cooper after many years of friendship. Douglas could be difficult but never did I hear anyone as vitriolic as he was to poor Kathy Sutherland. Douglas began to think that Graham was sacrificing his art to commercial considerations, at one time seeming to flatter the dreadful British Prime Minister, Harold Wilson, in the hope of being commissioned to do a portrait of him. In 1975, when Kathy complained that Douglas was not including Graham's work in a particular exhibition of celebrated painters, he flew at her describing her as a 'babbling, muddle-headed gossip . . . an evil, destructive monster' and writing to her: 'Sail on, sweet idiot, until you hit further reefs.' It was terrible.

In the middle of the row, we gave a lunch for Prince Rainier and Princess Grace, without realizing what had been going on. The Sutherlands came and so did Douglas. He merely nodded at them and said nothing. Kathy tried everything to effect a reconciliation, even suggesting that Douglas was on drugs for his ill health and that this was effecting his judgment. But Douglas would not relent. Their long friendship was over, and every time the names of the Sutherlands were mentioned, this produced a further torrent of abuse from Douglas.

Douglas himself had an apartment in the Monte Carlo Star

later on, so I saw him often. He had marvellous paintings. At one time people joked that he and I might marry, but that was not a possibility. It might have been amusing to have the pictures.

OTHER NEIGHBOURS

David Niven was a neighbour at Cap Ferrat in a lovely villa right on the edge of the coast overlooking Beaulieu. It was called Lo Scoglietto. David and Hjordis, his Swedish wife, loved this villa, but they were put out when President Giscard d'Estaing introduced the right of all Frenchmen to consider the first three metres of the coastline as their own. David thought he owned all the land down to the sea, which was just below his garden. He was horrified by this.

Every morning he awoke and seeing the sun shining, he looked out onto the concrete slab he had built himself and counted the stray tourists, who were lounging there. David waged a silent war with them. He established his position each day on the concrete and guarded it zealously. The 'squatters' as he called them would lounge around and then at lunch time they would produce delicious food and wine that upset David even more as he longed to eat it! He refused to surrender his vigil when lunch was annnounced at Lo Scoglietto and so food was handed to him by his staff, as if he was an animal in a zoo.

David became gravely ill with motor neurone disease in 1981 and decided not to go to Grace's funeral in September 1982. He died the following June. Today his villa, Lo Scoglietto, is a pathetic sight, completely derelict and gutted, covered in scaffolding. The present owners must have run out of money when redoing it.

Somerset Maugham also lived on Cap Ferrat, at the Villa Mauresque, bought for a mere £16,000 in 1927. He wrote many of his books there, working at a large Spanish table in an upper room with his desk facing the wall. He felt that his concentration would be damaged if there was a window, so, stoically, he denied himself a fabulous view of the Mediterranean. In the daytime he wore white trousers and a blazer, with a scarf round his neck, and in the evenings he wore a velvet jacket.

Enid, Lady Kenmare was a great friend, with an intriguing past. Willie Maugham nicknamed her 'Lady Killmore' as she was rumoured to have murdered as many as three former husbands. Enid was an Australian, the daughter of Charles Lindeman. She was said to have made her first step in life by having an affair with Bernard Baruch, the American presidential advisor. In 1913 she married an American called Roderick Cameron and they had a son, Rory. Roderick died the following year, and she then married Brigadier-General Frederick Cavendish. She had two more children with 'Caviar Cavendish' as he was nicknamed, and then he died, leaving her a second fortune.

In 1933 she married Viscount Furness, whose previous wife, Thelma, had been the mistress of the Prince of Wales and had consigned him into the care of Wallis Simpson. He became a drug addict and was found dead one night in the small pavilion near La Fiorentina, where Enid liked to play cards. The gossip was that he was taken ill there, asked Enid to get him his pills, and that she went into the house, locking the door behind her. Next morning he was found there, stone dead. In January 1943 she married the Earl of Kenmare, who was better known as the corpulent journalist, Viscount Castlerosse. He had been married to the famous Doris Delavigne, who committed suicide in December 1942, though they were by then divorced. He too lasted only nine months, dying the following September. Then there was another scandal in New York, when a man called Donald Bloomingdale died of heroin, which she had given him. All these rumours of murder gave her a sort of *cachet*.

Enid lived at La Fiorentina, with her son, Rory Cameron, to whom she was devoted. He was a gifted writer and a talented photographer. Enid was a tremendous gambler, who spent night after night in the casino either at Beaulieu or Monte Carlo. Some said she bought La Fiorentina with her gambling wins. Later they retreated to the next-door villa, which was equally beautiful, Le Clos de Fiorentina. Enid died in 1973 and Rory died in 1985.[*]

GRETA GARBO

On Cap d'Ail was the villa which the reclusive film star, Greta Garbo shared with her Russian friend, Georges Schlee. This was a curious ménage since in New York he lived with his wife, Valentina, who tolerated his romance with a woman who had been her great friend. Schlee and Valentina lived in an apartment at 450 East 52nd Street and Greta Garbo had an apartment a few floors below theirs. Both were decorated in very similar style.

In the summer Valentina went to Venice, where she had a young American lover called John Bassett. Meanwhile Garbo and Schlee passed their summers at their villa on Cap d'Ail. They often came over to the Leonina.

After Schlee's sudden death in Paris in September 1964, Valentina seized the villa and declared it to be hers. She later sold it.

Then there was a man called Cecil Pecci-Blunt, who had a wife. a son and several daughters, with whom he sometimes lived seemingly happily. But when he was in the South of France his wife did not appear and he lived with a man called Cecil Everley, who, so rumour had it, he had met as a store attendant at Fortnum and Mason in London, and fallen madly in love with. His wife was known in society as 'la Reine des deux Céciles'.

---

[*] Enid's daughter, Pat Cavendish O'Neill published a sensational memoir entitled *A Lion in the Bedroom* (Park Street Press, Sydney, Australia, 2004). In this she quotes her mother arriving in Australia and being asked how many husbands she had and whether they were all millionaires. Enid replied: 'Oh so many times I have forgotten. Of course they were millionaires, it would have been no point marrying them otherwise. Anyhow I killed them all, I needed their money and divorce is so messy.'

ROSEMARIE KANZLER

On Cap Ferrat from 1956 onwards lived Rosemarie Kanzler, who entertained extensively at the Chateau de Saint Jean, Cap Ferrat, the former Charlie Munroe villa, which she asked Stephan Boudin to decorate. The house was beautifully situated. She lived there with Ernie Kanzler, a very kind, nice man, who was madly in love with her. He didn't mind if she had lovers, which she did all the time. Nor did she hide it.

In South America, I had been proposed to by one of Rosemarie's husbands, but had not been tempted. Now Rosemarie was very rich. We saw each other sometimes but really only became friends when I was a widow. I liked going to stay with her in her house in Greece.

We came from very different backgrounds, which is to say that Rosemarie had no background at all. She had started life as Leni Ravelli in January 1915. Her father was an Italian Catholic builder. She was employed as a manicurist in Zurich when a rich client came in, flashed her ring at her, and said: 'Isn't it a pity that you will never be able to afford one of these?' Ambition was fired in her and by means of sex, love, foreign travel, multiple marriages (some of which ended in tragic – though not wholly inconvenient – bereavements), she more than acquired all she needed materially.

Rosemarie escaped from Switzerland and found her way to Berlin by 1936, thanks to a good singing voice. This was the time of the famous Olympic Games, and with her composer friend, Peter Kreuder, she was soon drawn into the Nazi elite. Kreuder wanted to turn her into a new Marlene Dietrich, and I must say she did look quite like Marlene. Though that plan failed, Rosemarie did sing for Hitler at Berchtesgaden.

In due course she turned up in Cuba, where she was in her

element amongst the rich foreigners, ambassadors and the South American playboys. The night sky rang out with many pistol shots, most of them on her account. Later she moved to Mexico.

In 1944 she became the third wife of Manuel Reachi, as I have already mentioned. Then she fell for Barbara Hutton's brother-in-law, Prince Youka Troubetskoy. Eventually she married her second husband, another Mexican called Carlos Oriani, a tycoon, involved in empire building. Presently he went demented and was removed in a straitjacket. They were divorced in 1954.

In December that year she married Fred Weicker, heir to the Squibb chemical fortune, which was enormous. Four months after the wedding he died, but not before signing important documents which effectively made Rosemarie a very rich widow. At the funeral Rosemarie noticed a huge floral tribute from Weicker's best man, Ernest Kanzler, a one-time director of the Ford Motor Company, and I believe a relation, who later organised the Universal Credit Corporation. Ernie Kanzler was a man who liked to clinch a deal. He bought Rosemarie an enormous Golconda diamond ring, professing: 'I feel engaged to you. And the day you feel engaged to me, you wear it!' It was a form of premature proposal, but Ernie did not want her to drift into the arms of another.

Some weeks after this gesture, she dined with Ernie in New York at Le Pavillon. Dramatically she pulled off her gloves to expose the ring, and from that day on Ernie picked up the bills. They were married in July 1955. Rosemarie had had three husbands in one year!

Presently Rosemarie moved Ernie from Detroit to the South of France, where she bought her fabulous property on Cap Ferrat. In 1967 Ernie had a stroke in St Moritz and became very ill. Rosemarie took against his German nurse and accused her of having an affair with him. The next morning the nurse was out. But he had never had affairs before, so he would hardly start when he was old and ill. He died later the same year.

Now an even richer widow, Rosemarie saw off the American

Inland Revenue Service (IRS), who settled at the Hotel de Paris in Monte Carlo for some months in order to investigate the estate. She set about collecting houses all over the world, notably in Greece and Argentina.

The story was not over yet. In 1971 Rosemarie married Jean-Pierre Marcie-Riviere, a young banker, whose wife had committed suicide. She gave him a million dollars to assuage his pride. The marriage ended in great acrimony when he left her for a woman of her own age.

In October 2000, Rosemarie produced her memoirs, which were privately printed. Shortly afterwards she went to her stud farm in Argentina, La Favorita. She was then 85 and went for her habitual swim. She wore a hat against the sun, and gloves against the chlorine in the pool.

Her butler found her in the water. She had died, and apart from the hat and the gloves, she was stark naked, her favoured style for swimming.

KING LEOPOLD III

King Leopold III of the Belgians was another friend we made on the coast. He spent his summers there, especially after his abdication in Belgium in 1951. The King enjoyed an uneasy relationship with his family and indeed with the Belgian people due to the tragic accident in which his young Swedish wife, Queen Astrid, had been killed while he was at the wheel of the car. It was not the accident that alienated them but the fact that he had remarried. The Belgians adored Queen Astrid and one newspaper in Brussels had a leader which read: 'Sir, we thought you shared our grief, but you buried your grief in the arms of another woman.'

Leopold's second wife, Liliane, was a friend of mine years before her involvement with the King. In those days she was called Liliane Baels. There was a young man in Hungary who wanted to marry her, but coming from a rather austere and grand family, he dithered and could not make up his mind between Liliane and his inheritance. Finally he called her and told her he had come to a decision and they could get married. But he had delayed too long. Liliane thanked him for his proposal, but said: 'I am afraid that I can't accept. I am marrying the King of the Belgians!'

Liliane's son, Alexander, was born in 1942 with a heart defect, which caused her to take a keen interest in medical aspects of the heart. She established an important foundation in Brussels to provide operations for those babies with serious heart problems, whose parents could not otherwise afford to save them. She is a wonderful woman, highly intelligent and beautiful and elegant. She arranges important scientific and medical conferences even to this day, and yet she has never been taken to the hearts of the Belgian people. She takes no part in Belgian public life and the only time she was seen in public in recent years was at the funeral of King Leopold in 1983, when she walked arm in arm with King Baudouin and Queen Fabiola.

Princess Liliane made friends with the American heart surgeon, Michael DeBakey, and he often stayed with her in the South of France. He is perhaps best remembered as the man who performed open-heart surgery on the Duke of Windsor in Houston, Texas, in 1964. In his later years Arpad often felt unwell and was much reassured by the presence of doctors of international renown. DeBakey was a frequent visitor and we also had a famous heart specialist in Paris who came down to see him. Naturally, we did our best to keep these distinguished practitioners apart, but one summer they met on the doorstep. Later I was told that they said to each other: 'It doesn't matter at all, but I think we should double our fees now!'

The presence of Michael DeBakey one summer saved the life of the film actor, Curt Jurgens, who was staying with us. Curt was a German actor who later made a success in films in America, notably *The Inn of the Sixth Happiness*, *Me and the Colonel*, and he was a memorable villain in one of the James Bond films, *The*

Spy Who Loved Me. We thought Curt was looking a little seedy one day, so we invited Michael DeBakey over to the Leonina to see him. He took one look at him and said: 'You are going to Houston at once. You must be operated on within forty-eight hours.' Curt protested: 'But doctor, you are down here. You are not in Houston.'

'I will be on the next plane and I will perform the operation,' came the reply. Dr DeBakey had seen the symptoms of a fast approaching fatal heart attack, and this saved the life of Curt Jurgens.

There were so many wonderful people on the coast in those days. We saw a lot of the old Aga Khan and his son, Aly. There was Paul Gallico, another excellent writer, who dressed stylishly and mysteriously in dramatic cloaks. His widow, Virginia, my colleague on the Princess Grace Foundation, I still see often. She lives at Antibes, but is often in Monte Carlo, helping Prince Rainier to entertain and dealing with many aspects of his plans and correspondence.

A dramatic era was that of the Greeks. Aristotle Onassis and Stavros Niarchos arrived on the coast in the early 1950's and they gave lavish parties. Their guests were extraordinary – Maria Callas perhaps the most memorable.

Later the Greeks seemed to leave as abruptly as they arrived. Now the great villas are owned mainly by the Arabs who do not impinge on our lives in the same way as they do not entertain. But still there are the Safras, who own the Leopolda, the Lawrences, at the Fiorentina (he owned Braniff Airlines, while his wife was a top Public Relations person in New York); there is Theo Rossi (of the Martini-Rossi family), and there is Hubert de Givenchy.

We entertained friends from all over the world at La Leonina. Orson Welles used to stay with us and on one memorable occasion he flooded the bath. Elizabeth Taylor was fond of the South of France and she came to stay with us too. She always had to have a man in her life, and some of these were not wholly admirable.

Paul Getty was another visitor. We had our own petrol pump and would have the guests' cars filled before they left. It is surprising that Paul Getty's car never ran out of petrol on the way to us. He drove a huge Cadillac and it arrived with as empty a tank as possible. He also had the habit of bringing sacks of dirty laundry for my servants to deal with. In Paris he stayed at the Ritz and always took a servant's room. Then he would call Arpad so that Arpad sent his car and chauffeur and he did not have to pay for a taxi.

In the winter Arpad and I went to warm places such as Africa, where I continued to shoot big game, or to Barbados and Nassau, where I liked to swim. Much of our life was regulated by the demands of the racing circuit. Horses had always been my passion and after I married Arpad, I was able to give this full rein. Of this, and my famous Derby winners I have already written.

We spent much of the season in London or Paris. I loved dining out with Arpad. Only one evening I remember was difficult. He was placed next to Louise de Vilmorin. Imagine! But luckily no 'Triple Crown' for her!

Our racing life took us to Ireland, which I did not know at all until we went there in search of a stud. After that, Dollanstown gave us an interesting Irish life. We spent a lot of time in Ireland.

There is something about the Irish spirit which is very attractive and completely different from European attitudes. They lead their life at a different pace, in fact such an extraordinary one that I often wondered how anything was achieved over there. I think perhaps that the world of racing and breeding is a life apart from the average Irish existence. As you travel through the countryside, you see rambling estates with derelict fences and overgrown hedges, and then suddenly you come to a beautifully kept fence, white and perfectly painted, with a lawn evenly mown and a gravel drive impeccably kept, and you think: Ah, a stud.

We were lucky in our friends, who greatly enriched our lives while we were out there. First amongst these was Aileen Plunkett, whose advice and little wishing chair had first brought us to the place. Aileen died in 1999 at a great age, and with her the last of a generation of Guinnesses, eccentric, unpredictable, funny, occasionally alarming.

Aileen was the eldest of the three sisters, all of whom acquired a great number of husbands of varying respectability and also, seemingly a great number of styles and titles. The younger ones, who predeceased her were Maureen, Marchioness of Dufferin and Ava, and Oonagh, Lady Oranmore and Browne. They were Guinness heiresses and they led full and interesting lives.

It was John Huston who wrote of them: 'The sisters are all witches, lovely ones to be sure, but witches nonetheless. They are all transparent-skinned, with pale hair and light blue eyes. You can very nearly see through them. They are quite capable of changing swinish folk into real swine before your eyes, and turning then back again without their ever knowing it. Or of putting the wrong words into the mouths of pretentious persons, so that everyone, including the victims, is appalled at the nonsense they talk.'

Aileen lived at Luttrellstown, near Dublin, and was a legendary hostess. We went to many parties and often found ourselves participating in extraordinary games, seated on the floor, or witnessing scenes that were clearly destined to continue into the small hours of the night. Sometimes we tried to slip away at about one o'clock in the morning, but invariably Aileen would catch us in the hall, announce: 'You can't leave now', put a hand on our shoulders and steer us reluctantly back into the party.

The servants were paid but intermittently and seemed to accept that it was their lot to work for nothing. Aileen herself frequently regaled us with a litany of grievances, explaining why she was utterly broke and how life as she knew it would soon come to an end. I remember leaving Luttrellstown on one occasion, deeply depressed by all she had told me and wondering what ever the solution would be to prevent her from selling up in abject penury.

A few days afterwards I was in Paris, walking along the Champs-Élysées, when I saw my hostess of the week before walking gamely along.

'But Aileen,' I asked. 'Whatever are you doing here?'

She paused for a moment and said: 'I have come to have my hair done.'

'But aren't there perfectly good hairdressers in Dublin?' I retorted.

'There is only Alexandre,' she said. 'Nothing else is possible.'

TWELVE

The Later Years

FOR SOME YEARS Arpad suffered from Parkinson's Disease, but we still continued to travel extensively and to see our friends. We were in London just before Christmas in 1974, staying at Claridge's, when he suddenly suffered a massive heart attack and died. It was 16 December and Arpad was eighty-five.

His funeral in the South of France was attended by a great many mourners, including Prince Rainier and Princess Grace. He is buried in a splendid mausoleum in the Catholic cemetery, a magnificent edifice that can be seen clearly from the road. I visit his grave regularly to look after the flowers and check that the gardeners are planting things that Arpad would have liked.

I continued to race after Arpad died, and Bunny has had some successes with horses of her own. But I sold Dollanstown eventually and latterly have had some horses at Chantilly to keep my hand in. But what excitements there were at the great moments! It really was marvellous.

We won the Prix Robert Papin and the Prix Morny with *Amber Rama* and the Prix Vermeille with *Saraca*, all of which were great champions for us. In the years of my Derby victories I was listed as a leading owner and breeder. In 1961 I was fourth, with three winners, five races won, and a value of £35,943. In 1980 I was listed second, by which time the value was £186,198. When I look back, the best horse I ever bought was *Discorea* for 450 guineas. She won the Irish Oaks in 1959.

My mother was still alive when Arpad died, and she lived near me in Monte Carlo. Princess Grace came to her 90th birthday party at the Leonina. She lived until 1981, dying at the great age of 96. She was buried in Arpad's mausoleum.

My sister Sophia lived to the age of 79. She died in Munich on 2 July 1996. She had been born in Vienna on 8 March 1917, and in 1940 she became the wife of Reinhard Henschel, who played such a part in my life during the war. As I have recorded, they endured many difficult times, including the sad death of their only son, Frederick, from a brain tumour. Finally they were divorced in 1958. Her life had been so tragic, never easy. Even at her funeral, matters did not run smoothly. Bunny and I went to Munich and proceeded to the church. We sat there waiting and nothing happened. Then an official came over and apologised to us, saying: 'Unfortunately the priest mistook the time and there will be a delay of forty-five minutes.' It was horribly symbolic of my poor sister's whole life somehow.

The Leonina had been left to Flockie but I could use it for the rest of my life. But I preferred to live in Monte Carlo now and Arpad had bought an apartment in the Monte Carlo Star. So I agreed to release the Leonina to Flockie, and in exchange she bought two more studios next to the one in the Monte Carlo Star, and I moved there. Flockie sold the Leonina to an Italian.

I sold Arpad's great collection of botanical books at Sotheby's in London and the pornographic ones in France. Occasionally visitors who stay with me in Monte Carlo are surprised to find one of these curious volumes in my bookshelves in Monte Carlo. The reason is that it must have slipped through the net at the time.

For some years I kept an apartment in Hyde Park Gardens, and also in 800, Fifth Avenue, in New York, but recently I decided it was easier for me to stay in an hotel, even if the service is nothing close to the standards of earlier times. In London I usually stay at the Connaught, and entertain there, or at Mark's Club, Harry's Bar, or Claridge's.

I still keep my apartment at the Avenue Foch, though Paris is really unbearable now with all the tourists, and so hot in the summer. Manners have deteriorated everywhere, but are still upheld by figures such as Andrew Devonshire in England, and the quiet courtesy of Alexis de Redé in Paris.

I have settled in Monte Carlo, which is my home all the year round. I like to travel though, and spend part of each summer at the Hotel du Cap at Antibes. I go to Baden-Baden and occasionally to the United States. I have lived a full life and seen many changes. A good party will lure me from Monte Carlo, and it is surprising that there are still some excellent parties being given. As far as getting about is concerned, the Concorde has replaced the horse-drawn sleigh.

I talk to Bunny most days on the telephone. She is very good to me and we get on well, though there is an element of healthy bickering in many of our conversations.

Look, this is getting frightfully boring. It sounds like *Jennifer's Diary!* Awful! I think I should stop.

Epilogue

BY HUGO VICKERS

Eᴛᴛɪ had intended to expand these last chapters – to say more about that rarified group of friends that she had all over the world – some of whom live at an extraordinary pace, and are exceptionally rich, but who somehow escape tabloid attention. There were others like the Reagans who would have come under her scrutiny. But in 2000 she suffered a heart attack, which greatly curtailed her activities. The only enjoyment this afforded her was that she found herself in the same Monte Carlo Hospital as Prince Rainier, and the two were able to chat together as they recuperated from their respective illnesses.

She was still able to go to Baden-Baden and was pleased to find a new friend, Chantal Grundig, widow of Max Grundig, of the German radio company, with a private plane to fly her up there.

Finally the nurses moved in, and she died peacefully at home in her apartment in the Monte Carlo Star, which overlooked the lovely harbour of Monte Carlo with a distant view to the Palace on the rock, on 29 April 2003.

Her obituary in the London *Times* (published on 1 May 2003) attracted considerable interest. One paragraph read:

'She would entertain at Claridge's or the Connaught, her appetite being prodigious, and she was engaging company. She expressed herself in forthright terms wholly devoid of political correctness, and any headwaiter who politely enquired if all was well would be rewarded with a torrent of complaints. She judged humans as livestock, describing the wife of a friend "as a bad breeder." Lately she had all but completed her memoirs, which were awaited with some trepidation in international society.'

Later that summer her daughter, Bunny, took her ashes to Schloss Steyerberg in Austria, where the Wurmbrands had lived for centuries. There she was laid to rest.

Sources

CHAPTER 5

1, 2, 3, 4 Eleanor Palffy, *Largely Fiction* (Houghton Mifflin, Boston, USA, 1948).

CHAPTER 6

1 Count Thomas Esterházy to Louise de Vilmorin, 20 February 1957 [de Vilmorin papers, Bibliotheque Jacques Doucet, Paris].
2 Duff Cooper to Louise de Vilmorin, British Embassy, Paris, 5 March 1946 [de Vilmorin papers, Bibliotheque Jacques Doucet, Paris].
3 Lady Diana Cooper to Louise de Vilmorin, British Embassy, Paris, 11 July 1945 [de Vilmorin papers, Bibliotheque Jacques Doucet, Paris].
4 Lady Diana Cooper to Louise de Vilmorin, British Embassy, Paris, 24 July 1945 [de Vilmorin papers, Bibliotheque Jacques Doucet, Paris].
5 Count Thomas Esterházy to Louise de Vilmorin, 20 February 1957 [de Vilmorin papers, Bibliotheque Jacques Doucet, Paris].
6 Count Thomas Esterházy to Louise de Vilmorin, 20 February 1957 [de Vilmorin papers, Bibliotheque Jacques Doucet, Paris].
7 Count Thomas Esterházy to Louise de Vilmorin, 1960 [de Vilmorin papers, Bibliotheque Jacques Doucet, Paris].
8 Count Thomas Esterházy to Louise de Vilmorin, 14 March 1961 [de Vilmorin papers, Bibliotheque Jacques Doucet, Paris].

CHAPTER 9

1 John Plesch, *János, The Story of a Doctor* (Victor Gollancz, 1947), pp. 11-13.
2 Susan George to author, 27 January 2007.
3 Susan George to author, 27 January 2007.
4 FBI Report [FBI document - 100-3450].
5 Susan George to author, 27 January 2007.
6 S.M. Ulam, *Adventures of a Mathematician* (Charles Scribner's & Sons, NY, 1976), p. 109.

7 Countess Esterházy to author, 30 January 2007.

8 FBI Report [FBI document - 100-3450].

9 Susan George to author, 27 January 2007.

10 *The Times*, 4 March 1957.

11 John Plesch, *János, The Story of a Doctor* (Victor Gollancz, 1947), p. 33.

12 John Plesch, *János, The Story of a Doctor* (Victor Gollancz, 1947), p. 542.

13 John Plesch, *János, The Story of a Doctor* (Victor Gollancz, 1947), p. 547.

14 Jeremy Bernstein, *Janos Plesch – Brief Life of an Unconventional Doctor*; 1878-1957 (Harvard Magazine, Jan-Feb 2004).

15 Frances Campbell-Preston, *The Rich Spoils of Time* (Dovecote Press, 2006), p. 46.

16 Frances Campbell-Preston, *The Rich Spoils of Time* (Dovecote Press, 2006), p. 63.

17 Dame Frances Campbell-Preston to author, 6 January 2007.

18 Arpad Plesch CV [FBI document – 100-3859-14].

19 Dr Arpad Plesch to 'Jus' ----, Dorset Hotel, New York, from Zurich, 29 October 1941 [FBI document - 100-3859-14].

20 Interview with Tim Boucher, 4 August 2005 [Pop Occulture Blog, Internet].

21 *Time Magazine*, 29 January 1973.

22 Interview with Tim Boucher, 4 August 2005 [Pop Occulture Blog, Internet].

23 FBI Report [FBI document – 100-3450].

24 Arpad Plesch CV [FBI document – 100-3859-14].

25 Arpad Plesch CV [FBI document – 100-3859-14].

26 J. Edgar Hoover to Special Agent in Charge, New York, 9 December 1940 [FBI Records – US Department of Justice – Arpad Plesch (Dr) – FOIPA No 906881-1/190-HQ-100-3859-1].

27 FBI Report [FBI document – 100-3450].

28 FBI Report [FBI document – 100-3450].

29 Dr Arpad Plesch to 'Jus' ----, Dorset Hotel, New York, from Zurich, 29 October 1941 [FBI document – 100-3859-14].

30 FBI Report [FBI document – 100-3450].

31 FBI Report [FBI document – 100-3450].

32 FBI Report [FBI document - 100-3450].

33 Memorandum re Arpad Plesch, 28 November 1941 [FBI document –

100-3859-13].

34 J. Edgar Hoover to Special Agent in Charge, New York, 16 January 1942 [FBI document – 100-3859-14].

35 Report from Constantin Fouchard, 3 May 1942 [FBI document – 100-3859-17].

36 Director of FBI to Legal Attaché, The American Embassy, London, 10 December 1947. [FBI document – 100-3859-40].

37 Leland Harrison, Security Division, Bern to Secretary of State, Washington, A-1046, 7 September 1945 [FBI document – 100-3859-35].

38 Leland Harrison, Security Division Bern to Secretary of State, Washington, A-1091, 18 September 1945 [FBI document – 100-3859-34].

39 Barnwell R. Legge, Brigadier General, USA, War Department, War Department General Staff, Washington 25, DC to Dr Arpad Plesch, Savoy Plaza Hotel, 59th Street & 5th Avenue, New York, 24 February 1948 [Etti Plesh papers].

40 Walter Winchell column, *New York Evening Graphic*, 11 June 1948.

41 US Foreign Service note from Madrid, 6 March 1951 [FBI document – 100-3859-54].

42 J Edgar Hoover to Jack D. Neal, Chief, Division of Foreign Activity Correlation, Washington, 15 September 1948 [FBI document – 100-3859-51].

43 US Foreign Service note, from Legal Attaché, Paris to Director, FBI, 13 March 1951 [FBI document – 100-3859-55].

44 Much of the above derived from Arpad Plesch dossier in quest of a French resident's permit [Etti Plesch papers].

45 FBI to US Embassy, Grosvenor Square, London, 21 December 1953 [FBI document - 100-3859-51].

46 Susan George to author, 27 January 2007.

47 FBI Report [FBI document – 100-3450].

48 Late Baron de Redé to author, Paris, summer 2003.

49 Alexander George to author, 8 October 2003.

Bibliography

If you have enjoyed this book of memoirs, you might like to know of other books in this field. These are Hugo Vickers's recommendations, obtainable via Bookfinder.com:

Arlen, Michael J., *Exiles* (Andre Deutsch, 1971)

Bedell Smith, Sally, *Reflected Glory* (Simon & Schuster, 1996)

Berthoud, Roger, *Graham Sutherland: A biography* (Faber & Faber, 1982)

Bothorel, Jean, *Louise ou la vie de Louise de Vilmorin* (Bernard Grasset, Paris, 1993)

Campbell-Preston, Frances, *The Rich Spoils of Time* (Dovecote Press, 2006)

Dempsey, Frank, *The History of Mr and Mrs Arpad Plesch's Dollanstown Stud* (privately printed, London, 1979)

Fromm, Bella, *Blood & Banquets* (Birch Lane Press, USA, 1990)

Fugger, Princess, *The Glory of the Habsburgs* (George G. Harrap, 1932)

Horstmann, Lali, *Nothing for Tears* (Weidenfeld & Nicolson, 1953)

Lindsay, Loelia, *Cocktails and Laughter* (Hamish Hamilton, 1983)

Livingstone, Kathryn, *Ysterday is Gone: The Story of Rosemarie Kanzler* (privately printed, 2000)

Martin, Ralph G., *Cissy* (Simon & Schuster, 1979)

Palffy, Eleanor, *Largely Fiction* (Houghton Mifflin, Boston, USA, 1948)

Pálffy, Paul – *Cinquante Ans de Chasse 1900-1950* (Montbel, Paris, 2005)

Pálffy von Erdod, Paul Graf, *Ewig lockende Wildbahn* (Bayerischer Landwirtschaftsverlag, Bonn, Munich, Vienna, 1957)

Paris, Barry, *Louise Brooks* (Knopf, 1989)

Plesch, János, *Rembrandts Within Rembrandts* (Simpkin Matshall, 1953)

Plesch, John, *János, The Story of a Doctor* (Victor Gollancz, 1947)

Shirer, William L., *Berlin Diary* (Hamish Hamilton, 1941)

Sternberg, Cecilia, *The Journey* (Dial Press, NY, 1977)

Ulam, S.M., *Adventures of a Mathematician* (Charles Scribner's & Sons, NY, 1976)

Vassiltchikov, Marie, *Berlin Diaries 1940-1945* (Chatto & Windus, 1985)

Vickers, Hugo, *Gladys, Duchess of Marlborough* (Weidenfeld & Nicolson, 1979)

Vickers, Hugo (ed), *Alexis – the Memoirs of Baron de Redé* (Dovecote Press, 2005)

von Studnitz, Hans-George, *While Berlin Burns* (Prentice-Hall, NJ, USA, 1964)

Index

Names of horses are to be found under their owners

from Es, 98-9; moves in with Be, 99, 105; keeps Es in ignorance, 99-100; divorce from Es, 100; on later life of Es, 100-1.
Husband no. 4 (Berchtold – Be) On Berchold [Be], 104; on Be family, 104-5; in Budapest with Be, 105; visit to Ankara, 105-9; meets Papen, 107-8; & woes of her sister, 105-8; returns to Budapest, 109; & sister's arrest, 109-11; grave illness, 111; loses Be's baby, 111; precipitous departure from Be's country estate, 111-2; arrives in Vienna, 112; worries about Bunny, 112; arrives in Switzerland, 113; in refugee camp, 113; affair with Dino Philipson, 113-4; divorce from Be, 114; places Bunny in Switzerland, 114; sails to NY, 115.
Husband no. 5 (Davis – D) Arrives in NY, 116; on marital troubles of M, 116-7; interrogated by immigration, 117; re-establishes social life, 117-8; takes job at Austrian Legation, 118; works for Gayelord Hauser, 118; & for Elizabeth Arden, 118-9; meets Deering Davis [D], 119; engaged to D, 119; on D's family & past, 119-20; married life with D, 121; contemplates how to dispose of D, 121; & D's absconscion, 121; dismissive of D, 122; & visit of Cecilia Sternberg, 122; sends Bunny to

Chile, 123; flies to Santiago, 123; & affair with Nicky Nagel, 123-4; in Lima, 124; in Mexico, 124-9; proposed to by William O'Dwyer, 125; & romance with Manuel Reachi, 125-7; on Bruno Pagliai, 127; on Max Hohenlohe, 127-8; becomes restless, 128; departs for Europe, 129;
Husband no. 6 (Plesch – Pl) HV on E's relationship with, 130-1; HV on meeting with Arpad Plesch [Pl], 152-3; returns to Europe, 154; on Gloria Guinness, 154-6; meets Pl in Paris, 156; & knowledge of Pl's background, 156-7, 158; meets Pl at Claridge's, 157-8; travels with Pl, 158, 162; marries Pl, 158-9; on life with Pl, 159-63; on Villa Leonina, 160-3; on Churchill's visit, 161-2; on Agnelli & Pamela Harriman, 162-3; on Bunny's party, 163-4; on Bunny's marriage, 166-7; on the South of France, 168-9; on Prince Rainier & Princess Grace, 169-73; & Princess Grace's death, 171-2; on board of Princess Grace Foundation, 172-3; on Lord Beaverbrook, 173-4; on Graham Sutherland & Pl's portrait, 174-7; on Douglas Cooper & row with Sutherlands, 176-7; on David Niven, 177; on Somerset Maugham, 177-8; on Lady Kenmare & Rory Cameron, 178-9; on Garbo, 179; on Cecil

Pecci-Blunt, 179; on Rosemarie Kanzler, 180-2; on King Leopold III & Princess Liliane of the Belgians, 182-3; on Michael DeBakey & Curt Jurgens, 183-4; on the Aga Khan, 184; on Onassis, 184; on Paul Getty, 185; on Louise de Vilmorin & Pl, 185; on Ireland, 185-6; on Aileen Plunkett, 186-7; on Pl's Parkinson's Disease, 188; on Pl's death, 188; later racing, 188; on later life & death of mother, 188-9; on sister's death, 189; on own later life, 189-90; HV epilogue on, 191-2;
Horses of Amber Rama, 188; Battittu, 24; Dinarella, 16, 17; Discorea, 188; Henbit, 23-4; Lady Sylvia, 17; Pardal, 17; Pretty Polly, 17; Psidium, 17, 19-22; Saraca, 188; Sassafras, 24-6, Stephanotis, 16; Tapalqué, 24; Thymus, 17
Plesch, Leonina (see Ulam)
Plesch, Marysia (see Ulam)
Plunkett, Hon Mrs Aileen, 16, 186-7
Poincelet, Roger, 17, 19
Porter, Cole, 168
Portland, 6th Duke of, 70-1
Post, Harriet, 111
Potocki, Count Alfred, 74
Potocki, Georg & Susanita, 124
Pronai, Martha, 112
Prussia, HM Queen Louise of, 29

Quetelet, Adolphe, 132

Radziwill, Prince 'Aba', 63-

1. Clendenin Ryan Jr.

3. Count Thomas Esterházy

4. Count Sigismund Berchtold